# My Path To

# TRUE
# LOVE

Journey to a True Self-Image - Book 4

This book has been published under the supervision of Prophet Del Hall III and by F.U.N. Inc., the parent company of Guidance for a Better Life.

Edited by Joan Clickner, Lynne Hall, Del Hall IV, and Terry Kisner. Cover Images by VRstudio/shutterstock.com and DuncanAndison/shutterstock.com Author photo by Paul Nelson Photography

Cover Design by Del Hall IV.

ISBN: 978-1-947255-05-0

# My Path To

# TRUE LOVE

Journey to a True Self-Image - Book 4

## LORRAINE FORTIER

# ABOUT THE AUTHOR

Lorraine Fortier enjoys a diverse and exciting career with the Department of Defense that has taken her around the world working with the military in support of our nation's security. However, the grandest adventure in Lorraine's life has come from her spiritual studies under Prophet Del Hall III.

As a student of Del's for over twenty-two years she has travelled the inner Heavens with him and witnessed countless magnificent works of Divine Spirit. These life-changing experiences with the Light and Sound of God, while often unexplainable to the logical mind, speak naturally to the heart and one's true nature as Soul. Lorraine has come to trust and rely upon this sacred communication. Following this inner guidance and integrating the spiritual principles Del teaches have brought her increased awareness and abundance, healthier balance in all areas of life, and what she has always hoped to find — true love. She found in her heart a true love for God, His Prophet, other Souls, herself, and life!

Lorraine lives in beautiful Nelson County, Virginia with her kitty Sunshine who delights in napping in patches of sun or by a warm comforting fire in winter, her pet rabbits, and "her girls," the clucky hens out back in the chicken coop. Her heart is full of joy, gratitude, and appreciation for the many blessings that grace her life.

# TABLE OF CONTENTS

Appendix

# Author's Introduction

Many years ago I watched a friend bring her husband a cup of coffee while he was busy at work. It was a simple act but profound in the lessons and insights it has brought me over the years. Back then I had a very different perspective on this than I do today. At the time I saw it as subservient; a duty expected of a woman by a man. I wondered why he did not get his own coffee. My view was coming from a low level, so condensed and narrow that it distorted how I saw the situation, like wearing a pair of broken glasses. This limited view not only distorted how I saw this loving act of serving coffee, it distorted everything — how I saw life, myself, and those around me. I was essentially blind to it all and had no clue. I was not aware of the ways this was affecting me or how much it was limiting the joys and happiness of life. Every relationship I had was negatively impacted too because I also had a distorted view of love. I did not know the real me, and I certainly did not know what would truly make me happy deep down.

That was over twenty years ago. I carried a lot of unhappiness and pain of the heart back then because this way of living and experiencing life left little room for love, real love. It also separated me from God and from my own Divine nature. For as long as I can remember I have been looking for love, many times in desperate ways or wrong places. As a child I craved attention, and dreamed of falling in love someday and getting married. As an adult I yearned for affection and intimacy, never ever feeling I could get enough. My childhood dreams matured into illusions and unrealistic expectations placed on those I would try to love.

Thinking back on the "coffee story" causes me to shake my head and think — wow. It is a reminder of how much my life has changed and how differently I see things now versus back then. I had reduced my friend's beautiful act of love and service to a gender thing and, in my ignorance, could not see the beauty and selflessness she demonstrated. We are so much more than male and female, skin color, religious affiliation, age, or any other physical or social label. We are Soul! Our essential nature is Divine because we were created by God in His image and endowed with Divine qualities. As Soul we are eternal and are given the gift of time to learn lifetime after lifetime; this is our journey. We are all on one whether we realize it or not. Our journey spans many incarnations in a grand adventure that will eventually lead us back home to the Heart of God where we were first created. This homecoming is not the end of the adventure however, in many ways it is just the beginning! Lifetime after lifetime we incarnate here in "earth school" to learn the ways of God — of Love. At the center of most of the lessons of living we encounter on our journey is an opportunity to learn about love and become better at giving and receiving love. This is the big-picture; the long-term view of Soul as contrasted with the narrow lower view I once held. From this view of Soul a boundless expanse exists. When we open our heart to God's Love, it lifts us to a higher view, and a whole new world of unlimited possibility and love awaits. We begin to see the infinite ways love can be expressed and appreciate all the ways it may come back to us, even in something as seemingly small as a cup of coffee. The size and packaging of the love that's delivered does not make it more or less significant. Any act, no matter how seemingly small, if motivated by love is special and profound. Love is love.

God's Love, Grace, and spiritual guidance through His Prophet, Del Hall III, have helped me grow from seeing through "broken glasses" to having the clarity of Soul. Having the privilege of being Del's student for over twenty-two years has brought me this clarity and so much more! I found myself. I found happiness, peace, and joy, and I found that which I have hungered for so long — real love. And now for the rest of the story... my friend I spoke of who brought her husband coffee is Lynne Hall. Lynne is Prophet Del Hall's beautiful wife. She taught me one of the biggest lessons of my life on love without ever saying a word. I don't think she knew at the time she was teaching anyone anything — she was just being her wonderful self, doing what she loves to do — serving. It was in ways such as this I was taught at Del's school as the Holy Spirit worked through him directly and indirectly. Because God's Love flows through him in such a pure way, Del has been my greatest teacher and role model of love for all time.

This story is about how my eyes and my heart have been opened to the beauty of true love. Its telling is a deeply personal testimony I share with you dear reader, because I want you to know what is possible, and because I want to share with you the reality of what a spiritual journey looks like. It's not about putting on righteous airs or pretending to be spiritual. It's about real growth and real gains that can be yours for eternity. It might look kind of messed up, broken, and hopeless at times, but that is all part of growing into who you already are and manifesting your Divine nature. I have been changed forever, and my life has been blessed in countless ways, sublime and profound because God's Grace led me to Del. It is my hope this story will speak to you in some special way and provide you a view of what is possible through God and His Prophet. That as a child of God, you too may find the love your heart desires.

# 1
# Precious Memories

"Can we drive all night Dad, pleeeaase?" This solitary plea would spring up from somewhere amongst the gaggle of my siblings, soon to become a chorus of voices, "Yeah Dad, can we drive all night, please?" We were on the road! A place we loved to be because it meant we were all together. My family was large by today's standards, seven boys and two girls; and all but one survived infancy. I was second to the youngest of our brood. My parents could not afford vacations involving hotel rooms, that was just too expensive. So my dad, who was a long-haul truck driver and very much at home driving big rigs, had the inspiration to buy a used Greyhound bus and have it converted into a camper. Marge's Barge, named after my mother Marge, was our home on wheels and how we vacationed from the time I was five until all of us kids were grown. Several years after graduating from college I happened to be at my parents' house visiting the day it was sold. Tears rolled down my cheeks as I watched it drive away down the hill. It was bittersweet; almost twenty years of my life involved that bus, and it had become part of our family's most precious memories.

I'm not exactly sure what was so special about driving all night. I think it had to do with the fact that truck drivers preferred to drive at night when they could have the road mostly to themselves and make good time to their next destination. The road was like my dad's "office," and driving all night was sort of like going to work with him. With his being away from home five to six days a week, it was a way to share the part of his life that took him away from such a big part of ours. There was protocol associated with driving all night, that too contributed to its mystique. It began late in the afternoon when we would stop at some roadside rest area along some highway in some state. We would have a simple dinner, go out to run around and play until dusk, and then put our pajamas on as my dad maneuvered the bus back out onto the highway into the dawning night. There was an unexplainable excitement to it I still feel to this day when I am on a long drive at night. My dad didn't often give in to our requests for such a break from our normal routine of driving during the daytime. He knew no matter how much we would say we'd stay awake, after a couple hours everyone; including my mom, would all be sleeping and he'd be left driving all night — by himself. But one time I did stay awake while everyone else gave way. I sat in a portable seat that was once a highchair for my little brother. The top half of the highchair had been sawed off to give it extra service-life as a stool. It was the perfect size to fit the little area to the right of the driver's seat, and it was the best seat in the house, usually reserved for my mom or one of the eldest boys. But tonight was different. They were all asleep so I got to sit in the seat! I sat next to my dad for what seemed to be hours, silent as he drove, swaying with the gentle curves of the highway… just me and my dad. In our large family one-on-one time with a parent was rare. It is one of the only memories I have being alone with my father when I was a child, and it was magical.

Forty-two years later as I thought back to that night I wondered, "Where the heck were we?" Where we were going apparently wasn't what made the memory special. I called my aging father, whose memory is now deteriorating as dementia sets in, and asked if he remembered that night. He did! Like it was yesterday, the memories flowed from him as he talked about how cute I was in my pajamas and long hair just swaying back and forth as he drove. "Where were we?" I asked, amazed he was able to remember. "Florida," he said. "I was taking you kids to Disney World." Wow — Disney World. The fact that we were going to Disney World faded from my memory, but the precious moments we shared that night had not. How on earth did my parents afford bringing eight children to Disney World, or to any of the places we travelled for that matter? How my parents managed to give us so much on one modest income of a truck driver with an eighth-grade education is a mystery to me. It fills me with tears of gratitude when I think of how much they must have sacrificed in order to do all they did for us. It was love. I may have wished for more times like this and not wanted our vacations to end, but one thing is for sure, I was loved.

# 2

# Sister Lorraine

My parents raised us in the traditions of the Catholic church and I went to Catholic school for twelve years, wearing uniforms and learning the rigid structures and norms of that religion. With this came some good and some not so good, but it provided for a solid foundational education that has served me well in life. It also helped water seeds in my heart I came into this life with that were already firmly planted. I loved God! I recall being a young child kneeling on the yellowing kitchen floor linoleum, in a circle with my mom and brothers and sister in our pajamas, saying our prayers each night before bed.

For years I wanted to be a nun, or sister as they were sometimes called, so I could be "married to God." Married to God not in the physical sense, but married in spirit. This is how I remember it being described to me one day by my favorite of three aunts who were called to be nuns in the order of the Daughters of the Holy Spirit. Something was indeed calling me, but it was "something" far beyond the outer social and political church structure. I realized this as I grew older. None of that appealed to me; it actually repulsed me in some ways. I wanted something more than the rituals, ceremonies, fancy robes, and lifelessly rote and memorized performance I witnessed in church each Sunday. That was not what was calling me. I wanted something deeper and more heart-felt, something more real and alive with the love for God I felt inside. What was calling me was eternal, and I had no words to describe it, but its draw on me was deep and ancient in ways I could not even begin to grasp as a child, much less articulate. As a front-toothless, snarly-haired, smiling little girl, being a nun was the only way I knew of at the time that could fulfill what I felt inside.

Later in life I began to question certain aspects of what I had been taught. Was I really going to hell if I sinned too much? Are priests more holy than everyone else? Are they really closer to Jesus and God than the rest of us? Do I need to go through them to learn about God or confess my sins? Do they know what is best for me? These sorts of questions were not tolerated by the priests at church, the nuns at school, or at home. There was nowhere I could go to have a frank and open discussion about what I was wondering. I felt guilty even thinking these things, and I worried about whether I was sinning by having these questions in the first place. Being good was important to me and not doing anything to make waves or rock the boat was paramount. There was no way I could let anyone know what I was thinking, ever. It was something I would have to keep to myself and hide.

I developed a tendency to push things down and not acknowledge anything that might be construed as not good, being disruptive, or going against the grain. My father was very strict in his discipline and quick to anger. Maybe it was because he was sleep-deprived or stressed at how to make ends meet. The little time he was home on the weekends he spent trying to sleep, which wasn't easy with eight kids in a two-bedroom, one-bathroom house. We would try so hard to be quiet, walking on eggshells in fear of waking him up, but it was nearly impossible. Sooner or later my brothers would erupt into some loud scuffle, and he'd be up with his belt in hand, kids fleeing to not be the first he caught. Luckily being one of the youngest, and a girl, I was never the target of his belt, but I watched my brothers get it a lot, and I learned to be good and not make trouble. These traits became part of my coping skills to get along in life, and although they helped me escape the dreaded belt lashings they didn't serve me well in other areas. I was afraid of repercussions from speaking up, so anything that might be met with disapproval was pushed down or ignored, setting up patterns of me being dishonest with myself and others. This was one of several ways I began to strip myself of freedom. So the very important and very reasonable questions on religion fell silent and did not get asked. I just swept them under the carpet where I put a lot of things I didn't want to face.

Unanswered questions notwithstanding, harsh realities of the religion I was raised in began to hit me like icy waters of a mountain stream as they played out in the news and in my own stark discoveries closer to home. There was a dark side to the Catholic church no one in my family ever talked about openly, but I eventually came to know about it later in life: repression, perversion, and abuse among its so-called trusted clergy. Fear and guilt-based mechanisms of control I had been indoctrinated with began to have light shed on them. Their hooks were so deep in me though, it took years to really see how they operated in my life and still longer to remove — and only then with the help and Grace of God.

I love Jesus and his beautiful teachings, but the living heart of the eternal truths he taught has long since gone from this religious path they bore. His teachings are as true, uplifting, and profound as ever, but over time so many of the man-made rules and dogma, church-created hierarchy and power structure, and the use of religion as a means to control people rather than free Souls, have overshadowed Jesus' teachings of love. They are no longer the main focus, or so it seems to me. The Catholic church felt dead to me. It was no more able to nourish me spiritually than a dead mother is able to give milk to her child. Over time I became disillusioned with religious things and began to reject it all. I became disconnected from that wonderfully innate love and passion for spiritual things I knew as a young child when I wanted to be "married to God." I grew increasingly distant from this part of me and drifted away from going to church. At first I stopped going regularly and would go only periodically out of guilt, but then not even the guilt or the fear of not living up to my family's expectations mattered. I just did not want to pretend it meant anything anymore.

This self-honesty was an important step in my journey. In hindsight, it was actually a bold step toward spiritual freedom, toward truth, and toward whatever it was that was calling me. It took courage, but I believe I was given the courage I needed as a blessing from God. Even though outwardly I was not having anything more to do with this holy-roller stuff, I think it may have been a genuine prayer through action and a signal to God that I wanted something more. I was answering His calling in my own unique way even if I did not see it at the time because it looked on the surface as if I had abandoned Him all together. This is why I have come to know it is best not to judge another's life, or even my own life, by outer circumstances because we cannot fully see the beauty of the seemingly broken road on which God is leading an individual Soul home to Him.

Despite all the shortcomings of the religion I was raised in and the circumstances of my childhood, I am so grateful for it all because it helped create the perfect environment for me to grow spiritually in this lifetime. It was all perfectly imperfect.

# 3
# Outer Esteem

For as long as I can remember I liked some guy, and for as long as I can remember I spent a lot of time hoping he liked me back. Whether he did or not had a big impact on how I felt about myself. If he liked me I liked me, and if he didn't I felt lacking and not good enough. As a result, I spent a lot of time feeling bad about myself, my looks, my interests, my family, and where we lived, wondering what I needed to do to "get him to like me." As far back as the first grade I can remember thinking this way when I liked a boy named Robert. The sun rose and set on him and everything he said and did, even the stupid stuff. He had a tongue-twister of a last name, but at the age of six I put as much effort into learning to spell and recite that long Italian name as I did learning the alphabet. This crush lasted nearly all of the eight years we were in elementary school together. What makes this more than a cute first-crush story is that he never really liked me, and those he did like became my ideal of how I wished I looked. It was painful for me when I saw the cute little girls he did pay attention to, because they all looked so different from me. I wished I was more like them and tried to be. I never let anyone know how I felt because I was too embarrassed, so I never gave anyone the chance to help me see how unhealthy it was to think this way.

At about the age of seven I started becoming self-conscious. My eyes were bad to start with and grew worse each year, so I had to wear very thick glasses. "Coke bottles" my brothers called them. As a cheerleader I was always at the bottom of the pyramids we built by climbing on top of one another. My rather solid frame made for a substantial base to hold the lighter girls up top. I saw myself as awkward and overweight. My brothers nicknamed me "Crisco" because they said I was fat in the can. This name stuck through my teen years into my early twenties even though I had started to thin out as a teenager. I was also pretty clumsy and had a tendency to trip over things a lot. My "two left feet," as my parents called them, earned me another nickname, "Grace." My brothers had a favorite line: every time I'd take a tumble they would laugh and shout, "Hey Grace, how's charm school?" I pretended to laugh it off, crying only fueled more ridicule, but on the inside I wasn't laughing. They did not know how sensitive I was. How could they when I did everything I could to hide how it really made me feel? I didn't want them to think I was a crybaby little girl so I tried to act tough. I know they didn't mean to hurt my feelings, they were just being brothers, but it reinforced the negative thoughts I had about myself. A silver lining to my clumsiness was that it gave my mom the inspiration to enroll me in ballet and dance classes, which I loved. I felt hideous in the costumes I had to wear for recitals though, they were not made for girls built like me. The costumes were made for tiny, more petite girls. Even so I enjoyed my dance classes, and I think my mom's plan actually worked, or maybe I just grew out of it, but I was not clumsy anymore. I fell in love with ballet and continued to take lessons on into my mid-teen years. I love ballet to this day. I love the way it flows and how it combines strength and grace. Set to orchestral music, it is a thing of beauty that inspires me.

My self-esteem was largely based on how I looked and how well I performed in things I did. Intentional or not, these were what set apart and got one noticed in the environment in which I grew up. I couldn't do much about my looks, but I found other ways to feel good about myself, like doing well in school, being a cheerleader, and learning dance. Being noticed was not an easy thing to do in a large family where noise and chaos were the norm. The only way to stick out in the crowd and get any attention in all the hubbub was *to do* something special. Just being myself didn't feel like it was enough. My parents were so busy making a living and caring for us that their time and attention was a scarce commodity that had to be divided many ways. For me, time and attention equated to love. I think the same was true for my siblings too. We all seemed to have a similar attention seeking streak in us that manifested in various ways. I wouldn't see it until decades later, but this self-esteem problem contributed to some very negative habits and led to destructive and unhealthy behaviors. Lacking a healthy self-esteem and being insecure led me to seeking approval and esteem from others by doing things to earn it. This may have temporarily filled a need, but the problem is that when it is coming from outside of you it never feels like enough. It left me wanting and being needy, burdening those around me for what should have been something intrinsically provided from within. It wasn't until much later in life when I met Del and he helped me see my true nature as Soul, that I would begin to love myself in a healthy and balanced way.

# 4

# Mixed Messages

When I was in elementary school I fantasized about being older someday and going on dates, scripting them to include first going to church and then going out to eat or going to do some activity. I totally bought into the "knight in shining armor" fantasy. Prince Charming would come and rescue me, take care of me, and provide love, happiness, security, and material comforts. Who knows where we pick these things up, but this was so ingrained in me I think it may have come with me from a past life as something to resolve in this one. I didn't even realize I thought this way until years later when repeated relationship failures forced serious self-reflection. Living life and being happy somehow became fused with being with someone. I couldn't wait until I was sixteen and old enough to date. It wasn't long until I had a steady boyfriend, and he became the center of my world aside from school and a few interests. We spent a lot of time together watching movies, playing board games, and hanging out at each other's houses. We dated for several years and our families thought we might get married, but I was headed for college and he was not, and soon our lives were going in different directions. I broke it off, and within a few months I was back in another steady relationship with someone I met at school. This time it lasted a year and a half, and once again I ended it. I started bartending because the tips were excellent and the hours fit into my class schedule at college. This brought me into the nightclub scene, and I started hanging with a different kind of crowd. Over the next couple years I was in several shorter back-to-back relationships always ending in disillusionment and disappointment. No one seemed to be able to live up to being Prince Charming. I craved the closeness and attention that came with being with someone and was searching for love I knew was out there somewhere, but I had no idea how to find it. I became increasingly quick to move from one guy to the next. Within three to six months, sometimes less, it would be over, until I met John and we married.

There was a time in my life when I was younger I thought I would wait for marriage to be with someone sexually; after all that was what we were taught by the Catholic church. Sex was only to be between married people to have children, not for pleasure. But there was a paradox going on in my life sending me mixed messages as I grew up. On one hand sex was taboo, rarely spoken of and shrouded in mystery, shame, embarrassment, and whispers. At best there were shy and awkward references to it when those who were well meaning, like my mom, tried to teach about it. At the same time though, it was a regular source of off-color jokes and innuendos at family gatherings from aunts, uncles, brothers, and even my dad. Being ten years younger than my eldest brother, these impressions were streaming into my world as far back as my memories will take me. I learned things most children under ten know nothing about, and I was completely unprepared to process the powerful thoughts and feelings that came with this carnal knowledge. As my siblings grew into their teens and twenties their conquests and exploits were the source of stories, boasting, and pride, unchallenged and unmediated by the busy adults in my life. It seemed the norm to make locker room type references in sporting and casual ways to what was intended to be a sacred act. The environment seemed normal to me, as this was the world I had grown up in. It was a world that was often very coarse and physically oriented and interpreted. It seemed everything had a sexual connotation to it, either overt or implied. But I looked up to my brothers in so many ways consciously and unconsciously; they seemed to know everything. It was mainly through interactions with them that I learned to relate to men. It would become how I tried to fit in and be one of the guys with those I met in college and in the male-dominated engineering career I chose, which caused me to send mixed messages of my own.

I shifted from being more aligned with the church's teaching, and my original plan of waiting for marriage, to being more curious and wanting to explore what had once been taboo and off-limits to consider. I ended up swinging from one end of the spectrum to the other. This is the way of human nature I suppose. In my early teens I was labeled as a goody-two-shoes in my family. My youngest brother once contrasted me with my sister by saying I was a country girl (meaning more conservative) and she was a city girl, in his attempt to describe the differences in our personalities and behavior, but this changed as I got older. One day in my early twenties he stated I was now a city girl too. I was struck by the perceptive honesty of my little brother. The reality of his words brought a subtle, almost subconscious grieving over the lost innocence and purity I once saw in myself, and later in life this turned into genuine sadness. I had waited nearly two years to become physically intimate with my first boyfriend and after that became much less inhibited. Yes I found pleasure in it, and I became comfortable and confident with my sensual nature, but there was more to it than that. I was searching to share something special and feel close with someone. I felt it necessary to accelerate a relationship to this physical stage in order to find the intimacy and love I was hopeful I would find. To compound matters, the poor self-esteem, insecurity, and fear of expressing myself honestly and openly through words that I experienced in childhood followed me into adulthood. Physical interaction became a way of expressing myself, feeling confident, and being in control of my environment. Looking back on this time I think I may have been seeking affirmation and esteem through this. I used to find it in the outer world by getting good grades and doing well in activities; I just replaced my childhood ways of satisfying those voids inside with more adult ones. None of this brought true intimacy or genuine love into my life however; it brought just the opposite —

mental and emotional turmoil and repeated disappointment as the predictable decline and end of another relationship would come. It was a vicious cycle I would go on to experience again and again like going around and around on a merry-go-round, always ending up in the same place. Against my better judgment I would get back on and ride again, always hopeful the next time would be different.

"Do not settle for shades or shadows of love." Words a great spiritual Being would someday share and bless me by, but this wisdom was still a long way from being in my consciousness. The "love" this beautiful Being referred to was nothing like the feeble love I thought of at this earlier time in my life. Love for family, friends, creation, and God Himself didn't really factor into the equation. I put no real interest or value on these other potentially profound ways to give and receive love. I had love in the tiniest of boxes, limited to only the kind of romantic love experienced between a man and woman in a close relationship. It was all that mattered. To me it was the pinnacle of what could be experienced in life, and the only road to happiness and fulfillment. Not to say romantic love is bad or cannot be a truly wonderful and sacred part of someone's life, but it was way out of whack in my world. Life for me was punctuated and measured by those times I was in a relationship. The in-between times were like downtimes or doldrums, when I was just treading water until I could once again be in another relationship. That was when life really happened. "I just want to see you happy," is what family would say, implying I needed to be with someone for that to be possible, and I bought into that illusion, completely. I had no idea what real love was, yet I sought it as a starving man desperately searches for food, content with even the crumbs from yesterday's banquet.

# 5
# There is More

There is a popular U2 song from the 80s that has the words," … but I still haven't found what I'm looking for." When it would play, I'd sing it aloud with lots of gusto if I was by myself. I liked the song; it expressed something deeper I was feeling inside. I wasn't sure exactly *what* I was looking for, but I knew I hadn't found it yet. I was blessed with much in life: family, friends, health, a good education, an interesting career, and material comforts, but still something was missing. From the outside it looked like I had everything one could want, but as nice as material things are, they didn't fill the void I felt inside. Life felt numb, and I was not happy with myself or comfortable in my own skin. No matter what I did and where I searched, happiness and what I hungered for eluded me.

After graduating from college I moved from my hometown in Connecticut to California where I started working for the Navy. I had an experience one day during a lunch break at work while sitting at a picnic table with some friends. It felt like someone gave me a knock to my head or a kind of push from behind, but no one was physically there. It didn't hurt but was forceful enough to cause me to suddenly jerk forward. It happened a couple times and had me a little concerned. I was in good health and felt fine otherwise, so it left me wondering. What was that? This wasn't something my logical mind could explain. It was both unsettling and intriguing. I had met some friends around that time who introduced me to offerings from different spiritual paths, and I read and stumbled about in search of something "more."

It was during this part of my life the spiritual seeker in me was awakened in this lifetime. I didn't see it at the time, but the experience at work that day was like a calling card from Divine Spirit saying, "There *is* more." The kick in the head was more like a kick in the butt to get moving on my spiritual syllabus I had come into this lifetime to accomplish.

# 6

# Something About His Voice

After five years of working in California at my first job out of college I came back east by myself for a one-year work assignment in northern Virginia as part of a career development program. While it may have looked like I had my act together, inside I felt directionless and anxious. I had no real rooting in anything or anywhere it seemed. I was in a searching and seeking phase of my life — though I wasn't sure what I was looking for. It was an unsettled time overall with lots of change in several key areas: I had a new job, new living situation, new city I lived in... everything it seemed was in a state of flux. This way of living was exhilarating and stimulating, but being alone also made it unnerving and frightening at times. My career was the one thing that seemed to have any stability, so I immersed myself in it and the hollow comforts it brought.

John and I had gotten married several years earlier and our marriage was not doing well. It probably didn't help the situation now living twenty-seven hundred miles away from each other. The main cause of the problems however, was me. I had no concept of what a truly loving relationship was or how to be a genuine and honest partner to someone. I had a lot of expectations and illusions about what love was. I carried a mental image in my mind, an "ideal" or Hollywood version of what I thought a loving relationship would look like: romantic vacations, candlelight dinners, expensive gifts, and lots and lots of attention. I was in love with the idea of being in love. The love I gave was a selfish kind of love that was conditional, as it always came with strings attached. I was expecting John to prove his love, and he did for a while. I cringe to think how self-absorbed and selfish I was at the time, but while trying not to judge myself too harshly, truthfully this is how I was. Maybe he had a similar ideal he thought he needed to live up to, or we each needed this lesson to work through some karmatic entanglement from a past life. For whatever the reason we seemed to happily let it play out through our three-year cross-country courtship, which included many good times taking trips and doing other fun things together. I really loved his family and grew very close to his mom and dad, adopting them as my own. His parents would sit and talk with us for hours when we visited, and we even took a family trip with them to Ireland to visit relatives. We planned a big wedding and took a dream honeymoon to the South Pacific, a place I have always been drawn to. On the surface to our observing family and friends it looked pretty idyllic, but once married the excitement and illusion wore off. After several years I began to see the real person I married and realized we were not that good of a fit; we wanted very different things in life. More time passed and the play-acting I called "being in love" gave way to the emptiness of reality. Trying to live up to an unrealistic movie version of love would leave us both depleted and very unhappy.

Now living alone in Virginia while on this one year developmental assignment for work, I was frequenting the new age book stores in Georgetown and Old Town Alexandria, attending various talks and seminars, meeting different people, buying up the shelves, and pretty much consuming just about anything on the topic of spirituality I could get my hands on. The spiritual seeker in me had been reawakened several years earlier, and I was busy sampling the religious and spiritual paths I discovered along the way. I was like a butterfly in search of nourishment in a blooming springtime meadow.

I was lonely, but even with all the shortcomings of my marriage I wanted to honor the vows I took, so I looked for constructive things to do on the weekends to fill time. I would scan local papers and magazines to find out what events and opportunities the surrounding areas offered. One evening after dinner, sitting on the sofa in the living room of the house where I had a rented room, I came across an advertisement for the Guidance for a Better Life retreat center in one of these magazines. It was a rather short ad toward the back of the publication I could have easily missed, but I didn't. I was drawn to it, and the way its author worded his offering caught my attention. I was immediately interested and called the number provided. I spoke to Del Hall on the phone, the retreat center's founder and course instructor. He told me he and his wife Lynne owned and operated the retreat center on their property where they lived in the Blue Ridge Mountains. Twenty-two years later I can remember our conversation like it was yesterday. There was something about his voice. I instantly felt comfortable with him. It was like talking with an old friend and our conversation just flowed. We talked about my love for the outdoors and hiking and how I missed the higher mountains out west. He told me he knew those mountains; he grew up in that part of the country. He broadened my perspective, as he would come to do countless times over the years, and shared how the Appalachian Mountains, while not presently very high, used to be a long time ago. He said they were once some of the highest mountains on the planet, and their ancient history was reflected in a more diverse, rich plant-life and geology than the younger Sierras I used to hike. He could walk from where he lived now, down the short path to the retreat center, and find over seventy different edible plants. We talked about the various types of retreats he was offering, but there was something in his voice that spoke to me on a deeper level as we discussed which ones were scheduled next. I knew I wanted to go no matter what the next retreat was. Back then the retreat center offered a mix of wilderness skills classes and spiritual retreats. I was very much the dabbler at the time and was interested in some of the general outdoor skills, that could be useful when backpacking, as well as the spiritual retreats. Other more specialized survival skills weren't really my thing, or so I thought in my limited, opinionated way of labeling things "good or bad/like or dislike." It turned out the next class was a tracking class. I didn't like the idea of tracking an animal for purposes of hunting (ironically — this too would change), but the draw to go to the retreat center and take the next available class was stronger than any judgments I held. Gently, Del pointed out I did not have to kill the animal; I could just sit and enjoy it or take pictures. Every word he spoke seemed to extend the horizon of the little world I was living inside of, in every direction I looked and in every area our conversation moved. I don't know how long we actually were on the phone, but it felt timeless, like a moment in eternity.

# 7

# Just a Tracking Class

Driving up to the retreat center alone and taking this class was quite the experience for me as I had never done anything like this before, but I was excited to go. The drive from the Washington D.C. area out to the mountains was gorgeous and was an adventure in itself, especially the last several miles up and down a steep, winding, gravel mountain road. I was open to learning and to whatever this journey had in store.

When I stepped foot on the property for the first time a whole new world opened up for me. It was April 21, 1995; meeting Del would change my life in ways I could not have dreamed at the time. He was a natural teacher and I was drawn to him from the start. He wasn't just knowledgeable on the subject of tracking he taught but very experienced in it and a number of other wilderness skills too. We sat on handmade wood benches inside the thoughtfully laid out three-sided schoolroom that had a kitchen area in the back. The fourth side of the building opened to a sweeping view: a large fire pit and seating area, the retreat center's pond, and sleeping shelters all encompassed by surrounding mountains, protected like a precious pearl. The retreat center was meticulously cared for with love. It showed in everything Del and Lynne built and maintained, right down to the plush carpet of gravel that had been freshly raked just for us. We started the first night with in-class instruction that continued the next morning. Out in the tracking field later the second day, Del encouraged us as we practiced what he taught earlier in the classroom by placing popsicle sticks in the dirt where we saw the tracks of the deer that had come through the area.

I enjoyed the class and found I had a natural ability to see the tracks in the dirt during our practice sessions, or so I thought at the time. Looking back, I think I had help from Divine Spirit who gave me the ability or maybe enhanced what natural ability might have been there. This boosted my confidence, helping me relax as a means of opening my heart. An open heart is where God delivers His gifts, and it is difficult to accept His gifts of love if you're worried, uptight, or fearful. I would eventually come to understand this at deeper levels and learn tools to help me do my part to make that happen, but for now all I knew is I was having fun. I was in a beautiful place nestled in the mountains, doing something new that I surprisingly just happened to be good at.

Being able to relax and just enjoy myself was an extra special gift because it wasn't an easy thing for me to do. I often found myself in situations where I was simultaneously drawn and excited by something but also frightened by it. In such times I would quietly undermine myself by questioning my ability to do whatever it was safely and capably. My insecurity and lack of confidence would put a damper on my enjoyment and make me anxious. The insidious nature of this habit tripped me up in all sorts of ways. I enjoyed hiking and camping, but I was constantly on edge wondering what animal was out there in the woods that would jump out and get me. I looked forward to crawling into my tent and snuggling into my cozy sleeping bag after a long day of backpacking and exploring unchartered ground, yet I would lie awake for long, anxiety-filled hours trying to relax enough to fall asleep. I loved looking up at the stars in the night sky away from the starlight-drowning beacons of the city, but I was terrified of the dark. I enjoyed the peace and tranquility of nature, but I was not at all comfortable being alone. Being alone with myself usually meant being with my own fearful, self-limiting thoughts. It was a counterproductive habit that was also very tiring. So many things easily frightened me while doing the things I enjoyed, but for some inexplicable reason I was able to do them anyway. Was it sheer willpower? Was I trying to prove something to myself? Or was it one of the thousands upon thousands of unnoticed blessings that quietly graced my life? Perhaps it was all of the above. How much more fun and joy could there be doing all the things I enjoyed without this life-draining fear? If only joy wasn't so exhausting.

After signing up to go to retreat at Guidance for a Better Life I worried about things like this, including having to go to the outhouse at night. What might jump out at me from behind a tree and scare me? But my draw to meet Del and take his class outweighed my fears. Maybe I was given a little extra courage by Spirit. Amazingly, while I was there I was more relaxed and at peace than ever before. I was not as afraid of the dark or being in the woods at night. I felt safer somehow, protected. I just knew I was in good hands. I slept like a baby on a bed of fresh straw in one of the retreat center's native-style shelters.

On the second night, after class was over and everyone had gone to bed, I stood on the grassy hill overlooking the pond. I was soaking in the beauty of the clear sky and the brilliant stars, appreciating the calmness and grateful for the courage I had to stand there "alone" in the dark and still be at peace. I became aware of a bright white light over my right shoulder just out of my peripheral vision. It surprised me, but it was a gentle presence that didn't scare me. I turned quickly to see it, but when I looked it was gone. I eventually settled down and went back to looking out over the pond enjoying the peacefulness, when I saw the white light once again. This time I turned slowly hoping to see more of the light and what it was; only as I turned around enough to look directly it was gone again. This happened once more but this time I didn't turn at all and instead used my wide-angle vision, as we were taught in class, in order to observe and be aware without looking directly at something. The light was comforting, gentle, and non-intrusive, yet it seemed to hold so much more. I wasn't sure what it was, but I liked it and I knew I was not alone.

The next day I mentioned my experience to Del and he helped me understand that what I was seeing was the Light of God. He said Spirit can come in many forms and one is light, and this presence is always with me whether I see it or not. This presence, this light, is also the inner form of God's Prophet. Out of great love for me, it chose to introduce itself to me in a way that would not scare me. I took all this in, and although I believed in God and spent years of my childhood in church and Catholic education, nothing like this was ever discussed, outside of what happened to the saints and holy people of the Bible long ago. It wasn't something that happened today, much less to people like me, but it did. As boggling and unexplainable as it was to my technically trained brain, I experienced it. This Holy Spirit of God, as I learned in later spiritual retreats, was offering to have an inner personal relationship and help guide me spiritually. In time, by nurturing this relationship and being grateful for its blessings, this relationship could grow. Sharing this experience with Del was so important because I almost assuredly would have talked myself out of it by the time I had gotten home, coming up with some kind of logical explanation for what I saw. There are no drugs (which I didn't use anyway), or alcohol allowed at the retreat center, so I can tell you that nothing of the sort influenced what I experienced that night. It just was what it was, and I was forever changed by it. I knew I had found something special and unique in this place and in Del. There was something drawing me back there, and I would continue to take a couple more retreats over the coming months.

The experience I had during that first tracking class was biblical in a very real, respectful sense of the word. There are many quotes in the Bible that talk of light and God's Light, but there are only a couple cases where people actually saw the Light of God with their physical eyes. In the story of the conversion of Saint Paul (Acts 9), God's Light knocked him to the ground on the road to Damascus, blinding him for three days and then transforming his heart and his life. God's Light has immense power, a power of love beyond our conception. I would like to be able to say I so fully appreciated the experience I had at the tracking class that I immediately became a dedicated and serious spiritual student right then, but that is not what happened.

On some level I did know I had experienced something extraordinary. Del had a way of explaining things that made it easy to understand, and I knew I enjoyed taking his classes. However, over the course of a year, taking two or three classes only adds up to about eight or nine days out of three hundred and sixty-five. The other three hundred and fifty-six days of life have a way of stealing the show, so to speak, making us forget just how amazing experiences during these retreats and classes really are.

There is always something to distract us in life, "the passing parade," things that seem so urgent. If we spend all of our time focusing on the temporal aspects of life, we never get to what is truly important; we won't have time to invest in the eternal. Of course, I like many others had to discover what was truly important to me. I would need to decide how much of my energy and time I would invest, and where.

# 8

# Spiritual Lifeline of Love

There comes a transition point for the seeker, or spiritual dabbler such as I was at the time, when one decides if this is what they want and how important it is to them. During the first few years taking retreats at the retreat center I typically would not open my journal much at home, if at all, to review and remember what I had learned in the previous retreat, going several months or more without doing much of anything with it. I would metaphorically put what I had learned on the shelf when I got home, but this is not an unusual thing to do. It is good to go at a pace that is right for you so as to not throw your life out of balance, and everyone's pace is different. If you go too slowly however, you run the risk of not getting enough spiritual nourishment on a regular basis and forward momentum slows or stops, ground that has been gained can be lost. This is what was happening to me. I was starving spiritually and it was manifesting in my life in different ways, including a chaotic time separating from my husband. Even though I did not see the signs Del could see them, and he brought them to my attention.

Clarity is one of the many treasures of Heaven delivered by God's Prophet to students who are receptive. A seed of truth may be bestowed in an instant but needs time and nurturing to continue to grow, mature, and become more clear. I was given a gift of clarity by Del back then to help me see what I was blind to, the connection between staying spiritually nourished with living a happy, peaceful, abundant life. Today I more fully appreciate this truth and have begun harvesting its fruit. I have made the effort over the years to put this fundamental spiritual principle into practice, until it became a way of life. But initially, Prophet helped me "see" enough to know what was in my own heart. Then I could make a conscious choice, if I wanted, to start being more serious about tending to my spiritual needs and being more consistent using the spiritual tools he taught me at retreats. These teachings resonated so deeply in me, my heart knew what Del taught was pure and true, even if my brain sometimes wrestled with it. This was something I wanted to pursue. What a gift it is to know what is in your heart because it makes it so much easier to follow a path that is right for you. This blessing of clarity sparked a change in attitude that must have been noticed, because Del invited me to attend a weeklong spiritual retreat with a small group of students called Spirit Week One.

Spirit Week retreats are for students who have taken the introductory courses and necessary prerequisites and want more. They are very small, intensive retreats held in the cabins on retreat center property for those students wishing to take their spiritual interests to the next level. These smaller retreats can be tailored and individualized to a particular group of Souls. Del hand-picks these groups as part of a process to decide in whom he will make a significant investment by becoming their spiritual teacher, beyond being their course instructor for the beginner level retreats and classes. This is necessary because a Prophet of God only has so much time to teach, and it takes years to help one learn the ways and truths of God. If a particular Soul is not serious it not only wastes Prophet's precious time, it also takes away an opportunity for another who is deserving and ready. The timing for any one student to be invited to a Spirit Week varies, and there is no guarantee that one will be formally accepted as a student. Invitation is a privilege and not taken lightly. I knew this was a big deal and an important milestone. I was excited to go!

Spirit Week One began on March 12, 2000. My prayer at the beginning of the week was to know Spirit more personally and know what I was experiencing was real, to know this deeply enough so that my logical mind would not talk me out of it. We learned more about the role Del now serves as God's chosen Prophet. He is ordained by God to speak for Him. The Prophet is God's living representative through whom His Word or Holy Spirit flows and has both an inner spiritual and outer physical form. A living God always sends a living teacher in the flesh to help teach the ways of the Divine and help guide His children Home. Del never forced me to accept this or tried to convince me of anything; that would have violated my free will, which he would never do. He just shared what he knew to be true and offered it up for consideration; much like how I offer seed to birds that come to my yard. I simply put it out there, and if they are hungry, they eat. I don't force them. Through the week I could feel a sacred connection growing between my teacher and I, and this relationship could continue to grow if nurtured. He said it would take time to cultivate, but developing a genuine love connection with God's Prophet was possible, regardless of the specific personality that had the job at any given time. This relationship with God's Prophet would become the cornerstone of my spiritual foundation and the most important aspect of my journey. He is not here to get between us and God but to bring us closer to Him. He is a way shower of sorts to help show us the most direct path home to God. The Wayshower is one of Prophet's many aspects or roles he serves. In another role, as the Dream Master, he also brings dreams. Dreams are an important way God communicates with His children. They are part of His language, the "Language of the Divine," which is also the native language of Soul. We practiced becoming more fluent in our native language during the week by learning to understand our dreams and by interpreting their messages to us, and through direct experiences with the Light and Sound of God.

In our Soul bodies we journeyed into the inner worlds of Spirit, or Heavens. While Del led us as a group, Spirit blessed us with personal, individualized experiences that were tailor-made for each of us. On one such occasion, Del was guiding us in a spiritual exercise that helped us tune out distractions of the outer world and go on the inner to seek guidance, council, and wisdom from Spirit.

We opened our hearts to God by thinking of things in our lives we were truly grateful for and then we sang HU, a beautiful love song to God. I felt totally safe and was receptive to whatever experiences and adventures might come. I could see violet and blue lights swirling in my inner vision. My eyes were closed, so I knew the light was not physical in nature. This was spiritual light.

This inner vision became very bright. There was a beam of white light that came into view and out of this came "golden threads." One of these golden threads was being offered to each of us. It was a gift of love direct from God. We were told that if we wanted, we could choose to accept it. I did. I reached out and took hold of it, tying it under my arms like a harness. I wanted to make the most of this opportunity, and I wanted this connection to stay secure. I knew what was being offered was priceless beyond my understanding and I never wanted to let go of It, or for It to let go of me. I thought if I ever encountered difficult times or got lost in the passing parade, the non-eternal distractions of the material world, this golden cord could be a lifeline and help me find my way back. It was a connection between my heart and God's Heart and symbolized God's extended Hand inviting me to have a more personal relationship with Him and His Prophet.

I didn't see it until later, but this golden thread or lifeline, as I called it, *is* the Prophet and my relationship with him. When I was shown this years later, the experience was enriched and meant even more to me. Del has been a spiritual lifeline for me. Our sacred relationship has blessed me over the years on many occasions when the storms of life hit, a couple which nearly caused me to drown and lose myself and my way.

The budding relationship with Prophet I felt during that first Spirit Week began to redefine what I thought of as "relationship." It was like nothing I had ever experienced before and was based on love, real love, not the facsimile I thought of as love. It was the basis for everything to come. Today I know my relationship with him is everything, though I did not fully appreciate the meaning of this statement back then. The trust I was developing in Del played a major part in opening my heart to a relationship with God. It was never forced or contrived, just allowed to happen naturally, like two people meeting and growing closer over a lifetime — lifetimes really. By the end of Spirit Week my heart knew I had been a student of Del's before in past lifetimes; the details and specific memories would eventually come, but I knew even without the specifics. The innate love and trust I had for him, which actually had been growing since our first conversation on the phone, was real, its roots in the distant past. The last day of the retreat he gave me a gift. A book called the *Rosetta Stone of God*. It is a book that teaches about twelve of the aspects of the Prophet of God. In it he inscribed a note to me. It read,

*"Lorraine, May the Blessings Be. So good to be together again.*

*With Love, Del"*

Del's note would be a tangible reminder of so much of what I had learned and come to know during the week. The experiences I recorded in my journal, the gift of the book, and his personal note inside would help me remember and give credence to what my heart knew when my head would try to talk me out of something. They were tangible parts of the spiritual lifeline of love I received from God I could hang onto — literally. This was so very important for me because the concepts of reincarnation, inner communication through dreams, and past lives were all so new to me and not supported by the religion in which I had been raised. Merely considering them felt taboo and foreign to my thinking at first, but Soul knows truth and I trusted what I had experienced.

While at the retreat center everything was so clear and made sense, but when I got home my mind would begin to chew on these things and cause me to doubt. An insight I received during my first Spirit Week was how wary, mistrustful, and skeptical I was toward anything that sounded like organized religion. I do not know how it came to be so strong an aversion, but I think it had to do with the disillusionment I experienced in my teen years as I began to see the Catholic church in a more true light. I felt betrayed in a way because I had such a deep love for God as a child, but these sobering discoveries tainted it. Walls went up in my heart to protect the beautiful, tender love I felt, and I think these walls manifested as skepticism and mistrust. But the calling toward my love for God never went away. It was what kept me searching, seeking, and dabbling with various spiritual paths until I found Del and his retreat center, or more accurately, was led to him. By Divine grace and fortune Del's classes, taught in an outdoor natural setting, sometimes using Native American ceremonies to deliver the message, were packaged in a non-threatening way that I was open to. If they were not I probably would have run the other way, fast.

As a true spiritual Master, Del works like no other teacher does. He knows his students better than they know themselves because he acutely listens to Divine guidance coming through him, having only our best interests in mind. Time and time again, until even my doubting, science-loving mind could no longer resist the evidence, I saw him be a perfect channel for the Holy Ghost, also known as the Light and Sound of God, and provide me exactly the perfect lesson, in exactly the perfect measure, at exactly the perfect time. No one, no matter how good a teacher they are, can do this on their own without it being divinely inspired, directed, and authorized by God. The more this amazing instruction was given to me as his student, the more in awe I was with it, jaw-dropping awe. And the trust and love between us as teacher and student grew. I knew this was different from any organized religion or spiritual path I had ever come across. The walls of mistrust and hurt slowly were dismantled brick by brick, retreat by retreat, with the most gentle understanding and loving care. Sometimes hitting things head-on and sometimes coming from a non-threatening, whole other direction, so the lesson could be delivered in the most productive way without going too far or too fast, risking my tender heart retreating back behind its seemingly safe walls of protection. I would struggle with this head versus heart conflict for some time, but would get plenty of help from Prophet on the inner and in outer meetings with him. Gradually all of the chatter and doubt subsided. I began to trust myself, trust Divine Spirit, and trust the precious love connection with the dear spiritual teacher and friend I had in Del.

# 9

# Karmic Chains Undone

Del is always teaching about nature: the nature of the physical world, the lower nature of the human consciousness, the higher nature of our true selves as Soul, or the nature of God. It is all spiritual, just sometimes disguised by the topic or retreat name. He uses every possible opportunity to teach in the most natural, kind, and unobtrusive ways. The eternal truths he teaches not only conditioned me spiritually but prepared me to ride out the rough seas that came when it became painfully clear my marriage to John was over and divorce was inevitable. The sense of failure was overwhelming. I felt like a failure. While still hanging onto what was and grieving the end of my marriage, I wound up getting into another serious relationship within six months of the divorce being final. The boost from a new person in my life was like a drug that helped me numb the pain and get over the divorce, or so I thought. In actuality, what getting involved with another person so soon did was delay the grieving process and coming to terms with how I contributed to the divorce. It also cheated this new Soul in my life out of having all of me fully available. Our chances of developing anything really good and healthy were nil until I worked through these issues. In His mercy and love God intervened and helped me let go when I was finally ready.

Divorce can be a difficult experience that may take one a while to work through on different levels. For me it was a process of grieving, healing, and learning to let go that came in waves and cycles. After the divorce, not only did I find myself grieving the end of the marriage but also an end to the times I would be able to share with his family, especially my mother-in-law and father-in-law whom I loved very much. It was like a physical death had occurred because one day, that was it, they were no longer in my life. They wanted to support their son and I understood that. One night Prophet gave me a dream experience where I was with my in-laws at a type of reunion dinner. Most of the family was there. We were gathered at John's family home which was very warm and welcoming. I saw his sisters and hugged them. They introduced me to their little girls who were too young to remember me the last time I saw them in the physical. During dinner I asked Mom if I could get her a cold drink. I fixed it with lots of ice just as she liked it. Dad said a mealtime blessing. I remember the feeling of joyous togetherness and warmth. I was so grateful for this opportunity to be together again and for how Prophet helped me work through this difficult period through dreams such as this one. He brought other inner experiences that allowed me to go through the divorce process itself in a positive and constructive way and be fair and honest when interacting with my former husband. This helped me get to a place where I could sincerely wish him well in his life ahead.

A major healing came while I was at a three-day retreat at Guidance for a Better Life. Del was guiding us through an inner experience where we were blessed with a sacred opportunity to visit Katsupari, one of the spiritual temples that exist in the vast inner worlds of God. These temples are a place where Souls can go to learn, be healed, gain insight, or have other experiences that help them in some way. However one can only get there if taken by an authorized agent of God, such as he is.

As Del guided us to the temple in our Soul bodies I noticed a sense of lightness, like I was flying, that I hadn't experienced quite in that way before. So although I was exploring new spiritual territory, I trusted him and did not hesitate to follow. I arrived in what looked like a large rotunda with many arched windows and velvet tapestries. Light streamed into the room from all directions. It was not ordinary physical light, it was the Light of God that illuminated the temple. There was a podium that looked like it would hold a Holy Book, but instead there was a fountain on it. John, my former husband, was there. He cupped his hands, took water from the fountain, and poured it over his head. I looked down at his ankle and heard four links of a chain that had been there fall to the floor. I went to the fountain and did the same, taking some of its living water and poured it over my head. He helped me dry my face, and we agreed all was as it should be as we journeyed separately on our own paths. I said goodbye to him as we left the temple.

This occurred nearly four years after our divorce. God knows us better than we know ourselves. Although outwardly I had tried to go on with my life, having now moved in with my new boyfriend Jeff whom I would eventually marry, God knew I was still attached to John at some level and afraid to let go of this first marriage. I needed help moving on. This experience was a healing one because afterwards I felt as if I was able to release something I had been holding onto. The chain-links falling to the floor made me think past-life karmic ties between us had been undone. I cannot fully comprehend all that happened, but I know the magnitude of the blessings were awesome. I felt freedom and strength, and I finally had the courage to move on. The healing waters of the fountain, an aspect of God's Holy Essence, originate at the Source in the Abode of God, the Ocean of Love and Mercy. It was truly out of God's great Love and bountiful Grace and mercy that this miraculous healing could take place when I was ready, and it was through His Prophet Del that this became so. At some level my former husband wanted this too and gave permission for this healing to occur. I know this to be true because Spirit would not have done it otherwise; it would have been a violation of his free will, which would not happen. I got a confirmation of this afterwards when I remembered John had a tattoo done the day of the divorce. It was a chain around his right ankle with several of the links broken free. It was his "divorce souvenir." I know he too wanted to finally be free.

This was an important turning point for me because as much as I tried to keep my heart open throughout this time, the pain, guilt, fear, and hurt that came from hanging onto the past had closed my heart in ways that were seriously affecting me; like a cancer cell, the disease was spreading. I am forever grateful for Prophet's inner and outer spiritual guidance that helped resolve the situation in a way that was mutually beneficially to both John and I. I am so appreciative of the ways he helped me keep an open heart where I could, soothe the pain and reopen it where I had let it close, guide me through the grieving process, and let go of unnecessary entanglements. Being able to finally move forward with confidence and being at peace with the past was indeed a very precious gift.

# 10
# Man is Not God

I lay on my small twin bed in a sparsely furnished room in the Netherlands where I was attending meetings for work. Feelings of gratitude for the thick down comforter that shielded me from the cold that awaited washed gently through my mind as I lay in that halfway point between slumber and wakefulness. I had been slowly coming out of a dream I did not recall when suddenly there came an epiphany as if Prophet intentionally sent me priority mail on the inner. "Man is not God." What? "Yes, that's right, man is not God." I heard him correctly. In an instant, a revelation came to me I had been blind to heretofore. I had been trying to make relationships with the men in my life be a relationship with God. I had put them in a central place in my life, placed them up on a pedestal, and put blinders on to any faults or shortcomings they may have had. I submitted myself and my better judgment to them in inappropriate ways. I made them my source of happiness and self-worth — a burden too great for anyone to bear. I set unrealistic expectations on them no mortal could ever live up to. They could never be themselves, have an off day, be vulnerable, or relax. I used them to fill voids and needs within me that were my responsibility to deal with. I had wanted them to take away all my unmet needs, hurts, and pains from childhood. I wanted them to fill my heart with love and never ever leave me. I wanted them to be God!

The sting of seeing myself so starkly and how selfish I had been was overcome by the joy and elation I felt at the truth I was given. Soul loves truth, and I think Prophet chose this time between wakefulness and sleep to deliver his gift because my mind and its defenses had not yet engaged, allowing me to more fully receive this gift of love. Here was a major source of my troubles with past relationships. How could anyone ever be good enough? These "lucky guys" were doomed from the start, and any encounter with me would end in disaster until I could see what I was doing. There is a wonderful and special place in life for a relationship with another. I know it because I have seen it demonstrated by some that have beautiful loving marriages, like Del and his wife Lynne. However, nothing should ever take the place of our most sacred and primary relationship, the one with God and His Prophet. In my unknowing and broken way I had it all backwards, but I was so happy to now see what I was doing. It had to be nothing short of suffocating to be with me — depleting, and miserable to be put in such a no-win situation. I felt sadness and remorse for those Souls I had wronged, and wished I could have time with them all to say how sorry I was. And my heart sang, "Thank you, Thank you, Thank you Prophet for loving me enough to reveal this truth to me."

# 11
# The True Vine

The scales of illusion were being lifted from my eyes by the Grace of God, and I could see now my misplaced focus and energy. Until one is right with God and that primary relationship is healthy and intact, I don't think it is possible to ever know true love. God is love, and if one does not know God he cannot fully know true love. He may think he knows it, but at best I believe there can only be shades and shadows of the real thing, or karmic love. Karmic love is what most marriages are based upon though few realize it. But the real deal — no, in my experience it cannot be done if one does not know the source of all love, God. And thus a new chapter in my journey began: to truly know, love, and be right with God. To better know Him I would continue to love, nurture, and build my sacred relationship with His Prophet. He is the only way to God, as scripture says.

On July 4, 2001 I woke up early and went down to the newly built addition on our house to pray and contemplate. I wanted to be near my beloved, as I had begun to call the inner form of Prophet. The room was so beautiful with many large windows and skylights that let the morning summer sun stream into the room. I loved going into this room because it felt so expansive, like my heart and inner life was becoming. During contemplation this day I felt as if I was part of a ceremony, similar to a marriage ceremony. The feeling of love that filled me was so special and strong. Spiritually, I was more fully committing to God's Prophet, a type of marriage. This was now to be the primary relationship in my life, not that I would forsake and abandon my human relationships, family and friends; this would make them all so much better. The ceremony marked another important milestone in my journey home to God. I knew Divine Spirit was always with me in the form of Prophet's inner presence, but this inner marriage ceremony celebrated a new level of commitment and devotion I had reached. My ever-deepening love connection was now coming into full bloom. This inner marriage commitment is sacred, holy, and spans time and space. It is forever.

On this day there was also an awareness unveiled to me. I could now see a truth that had been there all along — *I had finally found what I was looking for,* and that made my heart sing! Now whenever I heard the U2 song I would forever sing it differently than I had before. I would still sing it with gusto, but now I'd sing it with appreciation and love too. And I change the words to say, "I finally found what I was looking for."

Years of nurturing and loving instruction by Prophet continued, and my love and devotion to him grew beyond anything I could ever have imagined I was capable of. During Spirit Week Four in 2009 the depth of commitment and union with Prophet took yet another leap forward. After singing HU and sending love and thanks to God, Prophet brought us to an inner spiritual Temple of God. I found myself standing in the center of a very large rotunda inside the temple with Prophet by my side. He said, "Follow your heart." I had the sacred privilege of visiting this particular temple on previous occasions, but I was not sure where I wanted to go, so I asked him if he could bring me somewhere I could experience something new.

I began to hear the throbbing sound of a heartbeat. It grew louder, and then I felt it in my ears. I stood like that for a while, experiencing this beating and pulsing. I became aware of being inside a massive chamber. The pulsing was all around me. The walls were beating. I grabbed Prophet's hand because this was so new it was startling, and he reassured me. My body began tearing apart, stretching until it tore into shreds. This repeated five or six times. After the last time, the shreds went out to the walls and became grafted onto them, becoming part of the walls of this "heart chamber."

Slowly, liquid began flowing. At first just intermittent squirts with air bubbles then the bubbles went away, and the liquid began flowing through my parts, now part of the membrane's walls. Eventually my parts became part of the whole chamber, although I was still aware of the pieces that used to be me. The liquid was flowing through me the same as it was through the rest of the heart membrane. I was helping to circulate the liquid. At first it appeared silvery-clear, then gold. I was then aware of a blue tank-like vessel. My first impression was of a water tank or a type of pressurizing vessel that would provide a shower of water. I asked for clarity on what I was seeing, and the answer that came was that it was Prophet's true inner nature, the Light and Sound of God, the Holy Spirit, symbolized by this liquid form. The Light and Sound was going through the heart chamber, which I was now a part of, to the tank, and then filling it, creating a kind of reservoir.

I began hearing the music of HU. There was complete stillness, peace, and unity. I was. Just being. I realized I could not see Prophet and had the desire to see him and focus on him again. I was not sure where he was though. I knew he was there because I could feel his presence, I just could not see him. I began singing, "Prophet." I could see him again and looked into his eyes. We sat down, just looking at each other. Spiritually he came into me and then I went into him, even though he was already in me. I felt larger. I felt the top of my head going up and up. My eyes were wider, my ears were keener. He said, "See with my eyes and hear with my ears. See other Souls as I see them. I am always in you. You can trust this."

The next day, Prophet gave us an opportunity to share what we experienced during our inner travel to the temple, and he helped us better understand the deeper layers of meaning behind it. Sharing this way helped us gain spiritual wisdom directly from God's ordained Prophet; talk about hitting the spiritual lottery! God blessed us with these experiences and sent us His Prophet, who is fluent in the "Language of the Divine" and qualified like no other, to help one understand the significance and personal value contained within the experiences with which they are blessed. He helped me understand the reason I could not see him for a time was probably because I was inside him spiritually, symbolized by the large "heart chamber" I experienced. The grafting onto the walls of the chamber was in a real sense coming into union with the Prophet, who is the living Tree of Life and True Vine, helping to distribute the light and sound and blessings of God to His children.

In the Bible (John 15:1-11), Jesus taught about being the true vine and abiding in him. He tells us he is the true vine and his Father is the husbandman or vinedresser. The branches cannot bear fruit by themselves, they must abide in the vine. If we abide in him and him in us, the vine's life juices (the Holy Spirit, the Light and Sound) can flow through and nourish us and bring abundance. The branches bear fruit, or they wither and die and are cast into the fire. But when we abide in him we bear much fruit! His joy is in us and our joy is full — life more abundant, as promised in John 10:10. What was true then is still true today.

I was part of the inner body of Prophet. My body ripping apart multiple times was for the different sheaths or bodies (physical, astral, causal, mental, etheric) that shroud and encompass the real me, Soul. Each of these bodies ripping apart signified the "grafting" that happened at all levels. I know this because there was a certain completeness about it. It has brought new life to my relationship with Prophet, and I have a richer, more intimate, and personal experience of what it means to abide in him. Having had my bodies and my essence torn apart and merged with his, having had the experience and awareness of his essence, the Light and Sound, coursing through me, has taken the phrase I sometimes say in the mornings, "Prophet, abide in me this day as I abide in you," to a whole new level. To be able to remember, re-experience, and renew when I say these words has brought me a deeper sense of union with him that fortifies me.

In the days that followed we had more teachings on actual grafting which provided even more layers of understanding to my experience. Once again, Prophet was helping me integrate this sacred blessing into my consciousness so it could bless all aspects of my daily life. I learned that when a spiritual graft is done, it is done so some of the properties and qualities of the one (the root stock) are inherited by the other (the branch), but the branch retains its original qualities (gifts, talents, and individuality) as well. Symbolically, Prophet is the rootstock and I am the branch grafted onto him. It is like the best of both coming together, the Prophet and I. The graft is everything! It is our means not just to a more abundant life, but is our very connection with life itself. A branch, symbolizing each of us as individual Souls, can live for a short time in a temporary container of water to give it life and nourishment, but eventually the branch must get grafted onto a root stock or it will wither and die. The same is true for us; eventually we need to find nourishment from God or we will wither spiritually. Not all grafts take and are very fragile in the beginning. Grafting is not a onetime event. It is a process. Each time I go to the retreat center, each spiritual retreat, each opportunity to be in the presence of the Prophet, the graft is strengthened and made more permanent. Quite possibly I have been grafting over many lifetimes. Using this metaphor for what I experienced as uniting and becoming part of the body of the Prophet, means this sacred gift is not guaranteed to become permanent unless it is nurtured. Peace in my heart, and awareness, appreciation, and love for Prophet are what have been nurturing this incredible gift (the graft) and will continue to strengthen it to help it eventually become permanent. When the graft is permanent and union with the Prophet complete, then one finds permanent entry into the Kingdom of Heaven and eternal life!

# 12
# Emotional War Zone

This might be a good place in the story to restate something I shared in the beginning of the book; a spiritual journey can look kind of messed up, broken, and hopeless at times, but that is all part of growing into who you already are and manifesting your Divine nature. After such an amazing experience of unity and oneness with the inner Prophet, the true vine in which I abide, during Spirit Week Four you might think the rest of my journey was like a stroll in a mountain meadow. Not so. In fact, some of my toughest days and darkest nights were just around the corner.

After my first marriage to John ended and I met Jeff I was committed to being a better partner, but I hadn't given myself much time to grow and learn from those lessons before jumping back in and getting involved with someone new. In hindsight, by not facing things head-on and instead choosing to numb the pain of the divorce, I delayed my learning from it. I had already begun remaking the same mistakes by the time I even realized what they were, unknowingly doing damage to this new relationship in spite of wanting to be a better partner this time. I was still very conditional about giving of myself. While I was beginning to learn more about love through classes Prophet taught, through his example, and through direct experiences with the Light and Sound of God he gave, I still held many of the same misconceptions and unrealistic expectations I had before, and I still held the illusion there was some sort of "ideal" out there. I was still pretty much in the same shape in this regard as I had always been, largely because I delayed my learning and growth from the lesson in living I had just been given. Jeff and I had been living together for four years before I was ready to receive the truth Prophet revealed to me about my wanting "man to be God" during my business trip to the Netherlands. I had been trying to build a relationship with Jeff on a weak and shaky foundation, using old ways and behaviors that contributed to failure once before. It was a major liability I incurred by not giving myself adequate time in between these relationships. If I had, it would have allowed Prophet to teach me how to do it better next time.

It wasn't all or nothing though — my life was growing more abundant and was blessed in many ways even though I bumbled into this next part of my life much less prepared than I could have been; one of those blessings was meeting Jeff. He and I met at work, and we clicked right from our first lunch together as I learned he lived a while in Alaska as a child, somewhere I had always wanted to go. We shared interests in hiking, backpacking, and adventure travel to off-the-beaten path kind of places. We worked very well together as a team when we encountered challenging or potentially dangerous situations in these remote locations. One such time occurred while backpacking a one hundred-mile trek on Mt.

Rainier's Wonderland Trail. After a cold and rainy five-day period most of our clothes and gear were wet or damp; thankfully our sleeping bags and night clothes were dry. As we stopped to make camp for the night I became chilled as the high-mountain temperatures dropped. I couldn't seem to stop shivering once I stopped moving no matter how much I tried. In the pouring down rain, Jeff lit the camp stove and boiled water for some instant chicken noodle soup and then crawled into the sleeping bag we had zipped together to use his body heat to help warm me up. Another day, I had the chance to help him after a particularly grueling climb when the cold and exertion had depleted his energy stores. I helped get him comfortable, pitched camp, and got some hot food into him, enabling him to replenish with a good night's rest. We worked as a team like this in many things we did.

Jeff was different though; he would not play into my Prince Charming illusion. He was a take me or leave me type of person which caused me to have to decide if I could be happy with who he was, and although it was frustrating he was actually helping me to start lightening up on the illusion and look more at the real him instead of my fantasy. He had a lot of qualities I liked, and I admired him in many ways. We didn't fight much at all. Not fighting is also not making waves or talking about things when conflicts arise — not a good thing. I have since learned genuine intimacy requires two people being willing to be open and honest about their feelings, feeling safe enough to be vulnerable and trusting love will still be there and won't be withdrawn just because a conflict arises. Neither of us were skilled in this and really had none of these factors working in our favor. In fact, we avoided the conflicts to "keep peace" but did so at the expense of truth and self-honesty. Perhaps one of our most fatal errors. There were some things I disliked, but I thought maybe he could change over time. After living together five years I was still questioning if I wanted to get married even as we started talking about it and making plans. I once wrote to Prophet asking his advice and how to know if one was ready for marriage. Paraphrasing his response he basically said, if you have to ask then you aren't ready. It should be something you are so sure about you couldn't imagine not doing it. I didn't feel this way, but I also didn't trust myself and my little voice inside. Maybe I was just scared and gun-shy? I delayed the wedding for a year hoping to become more sure. There were a few issues that had always been there, and we routinely found ourselves hitting up against them time and again, but we did not talk them through. Nevertheless, we did get married for better or worse.

After marrying I settled in and really tried my best to make our marriage work. All along I was trying to live the spiritual tools and lessons I was being taught and trying to put them into action. I was learning so much, and my heart was changing, as God's Light and Sound, His Love, was transforming me gradually from the inside out. I was becoming less selfish and more giving, and though some of the earlier tendencies were still at play they were nothing like they had been, fading more and more into the background as my true nature as Soul was emerging. But I still had fears about addressing issues and would sweep things under the carpet as I always did. I didn't feel safe sharing my innermost thoughts and concerns. I feared repercussions from speaking up as I did when I was younger. I worried that I would not be loved if I made trouble and raised controversial topics I knew would upset him. I also failed to provide a safe place for him to share his innermost thoughts and feelings, concerns, and gripes with me. Things worsened and the bump under the carpet was getting too large to ignore. Unskillfully, I tried to navigate into those dicey waters I knew would rock the boat in spite of not feeling safe. I tried to be honest and share my inner world, but it was too late, too much damage had been done, and I had lost his trust in that regard long ago. His own tender heart was well fortified and guarded by this time against the hurts I had sent his way. I don't know if he saw or felt anything change over time in me or not. If he did, he did not say anything about it, and it didn't result in him wanting to take any chance at intimacy with me. So as long as I avoided the minefield of intimacy life was good. We were like really good roommates and made great companions, so long as we kept the peace.

Life went on. More trips, more adventures, stimulating work experiences we shared, and pleasant nights at home hanging out with our cats we loved. But I grew more and more lonely just being companions. As I continued to change inwardly, I wanted more than ever to experience a deeper level of intimacy and commitment, to love at a new level. I so wanted to share this with Jeff and tried in various ways: books, counseling, and inviting him to take retreats and classes with me. He tried each to a degree, but they weren't right for him and ultimately he said he was more or less content with the relationship we had. He was right: it wasn't bad in some respects, but it left me lonely and prone to crying in the night feeling trapped. I imagined what it would feel like in forty years after having settled for so much less than what my heart wanted. I saw myself sad and bitter and knew I did not want that.

During Spirit Week Four, the same retreat I was blessed with grafting onto the True Vine, which brought me to a whole new level in my spiritual marriage to the inner Prophet, I also came to know my own heart more. I wanted to experience something deeper in my outer marriage too. It was such a precious place to be spiritually and I wanted the same for my earthly marriage. I had to talk to Jeff and let him know where I was at; I could no longer pretend what we had was enough. I had dreams and insights during this retreat to help me gain clarity and be sure I was ready to rock the boat. I knew there would be consequences, but truth was becoming more valuable to me over time as was self-honesty. It just got to a point that those qualities were more important to manifest in my life than the empty peace that came with walking on eggshells. I spoke to him after the retreat about what was in my heart and how I wanted something more for us. I let him know how serious this was and that we had to do something, or I could not see how I could continue in this marriage. He needed to know I was nearing the end of trying with things as they were. I hoped he would want to join me in creating a new chapter for us.

A few months after this I was selected to lead a special project for work that required me to be away for four months deployed to Iraq and Afghanistan. I felt in my heart this time apart was either going to make or break us; it could go either way. It turned out to be the latter, and while gone it became clear it wasn't going to work for us. When I got home we separated.

The time in Afghanistan impacted me emotionally in a significant way. I have come to realize I am a very sensitive person, can be hurt easily, and feel things deeply. While deployed not only was I dealing with coming to terms with the inevitable end of my second marriage, I was also dealing with the heightened senses of alertness being in an active war zone. All of this wore on me, and I had to lean on Prophet to a very great degree to stay somewhat balanced. The days became months and our work was almost complete. As we prepared to return home, mixed emotions swirled inside of me. I was excited to see my mom and dad, family, and friends, but part of me wanted to stay and do more. I had made strong bonds with those on my team, and we would be going our separate ways soon. I witnessed the amazing bravery and courage of the men and women in our military, but I could see the dangerous impacts politics were having on their effectiveness and safety. I was grateful for their contributions and sacrifice but very angry at the rules of engagement that tied their hands, and often got them killed. I was conflicted over our nation's involvement in ancient tribal disputes we would never resolve by being there, but I love our country and its foundation of God-given liberty and freedom. I questioned whether it was all worth it. What were we preserving and protecting by being there?

These thoughts and feelings followed me home. I was overly sensitive to the news reports from that area, and I found myself crying a lot for no apparent reason. I was not alone though; Prophet helped me through this turbulent time. He helped me understand one may be physically or spiritually strong, but if out of balance emotionally, one could spiral downward and lose everything. It was a process, but he helped me regain emotional stability over the next six months through his love and guidance during inner spiritual experiences, insights he brought during contemplation, in dreams, and very importantly, being in his physical presence during retreats at the retreat center.

One day during contemplation and prayer he showed me visually what was going on. I observed a scene where we were walking together through a dense forest. It was dark outside, but I did not feel that same darkness inside of me. There was no apparent path or trail, but by focusing on the Prophet I knew I would be alright. I had a knowingness that he would lead me out of the dark woods into the light. This spoke to me deeply. The dense forest was symbolic of my conflicted feelings and emotions, but at my core, deeper than the emotion, I was fine. Prophet gave me a broader view of the situation, and this brought me hope and strength to continue walking through what I was feeling. If I were on my own I would almost surely have gotten stuck there, and it was a dangerous place to be by oneself. Del tells a parable to teach about this he calls the "horseshoe nail" story. There once was a brave and skilled warrior on a horse who was going into battle to save the kingdom. Unbeknownst to him his horse had one small nail missing from its shoe. Because of this missing nail the horse's shoe eventually came loose and fell away. The horse was injured running without anything to protect its hoof, became lame and collapsed, bringing the warrior to the ground. The enemy saw this and took advantage of the situation and killed the warrior. The warrior's death turned the tide of the battle due to the loss of this warrior's great skills, and the battle for the kingdom was lost. The punch line being something as small as a single horseshoe nail lost an entire kingdom. In this case the horseshoe nail was my emotions. Applying this to Prophet's parable it shows the importance of staying balanced, and in particular emotionally balanced. Emotions can erupt and in an instant change a life in ways one might regret. Not to repress them, but keep them in a healthy balance. It takes time and practice, but with the tools he teaches it is very doable. I believe without Prophet in my life I would have been lost in the emotional inner turmoil and sadness I felt back then, like so many others returning from the war affected by this. Others saw and experienced far, far worse, for far longer than I. I have such deep appreciation and love for Prophet, that he was in my heart and by my side every step of the way, helping me let go of the negative emotions and thoughts that had me entangled.

After several months of being separated Jeff and I got back together again and tried to make things work. We even restated our wedding vows together in private at home. We tried counseling again, but he was not motivated toward it and after another year we separated for good and divorced. Jeff gave me the greatest gift one evening when he said he just didn't feel like trying anymore. This was one of the most honest moments I could recall with him, and it was also heartbreaking because I knew I couldn't make this work by myself. It would take both of us. He was content with what we had and I was not. Really no fault of his own. When we got together I was a very different person. Having a deeper intimacy frightened me so much I could barely say the word. It wasn't something I sought. I, too, was content with what we had for many years. Even though there was conflict it was quite nice. But I changed and with that change our marriage would too need to undergo change if it were to survive. Even with the sad outcome though, I am ever grateful for his gift of honesty and truth because then I could do what was best for me (and I think both of us ultimately) now that I knew. Funny, one of our most intimate and honest moments came at the end of our marriage. It was something that allowed a real friendship, more genuine love, and goodwill to remain between us for many years hence. Despite the pain and grief that would eventually come and need once again to be processed, I respected his choice and appreciated his telling me so I could move on with my life. Jeff is a wonderful man, and I am thankful to have shared this part of my life with him. My life has been blessed by knowing him.

# 13

# Deliver Us From Evil

"I don't see how you can recover from this. You have been snake bit, and it is just a matter of time before you are gone. Maybe six months, I doubt you will be here in a year." His words ripped through me like a hot knife and caused my heart to race as my mind desperately searched for a way out of this mess I had gotten myself into. Everything I cared about seemed to be slipping away in the moments it took for the reality of those words to sink in. How did I let this happen? Del was talking about my actions and choices over the past year and a half that were cause to disqualify me from any further study under his guidance. I had just gone too far with my repeated poor choices, lack of discernment, and ignoring the inner guidance he tried to give. These led to losing my ability to hear Prophet's inner communications and see clearly, sending me into a tailspin, quickly spiraling downward. I sat there numb like a paralyzed mouse bitten by a venomous snake who had lost its senses.

In that moment the thought of not being allowed back at the retreat center to continue my spiritual studies was a fate worse than physical death. After seventeen years attending retreats at Guidance for a Better Life, I had gone from a spiritual dabbler, to seeker, to serious spiritual student. I had grown in many ways, and my life was blessed with grace and abundance. Regular attendance at retreats had become a priority in life, but my actions of late spoke differently. As with any school of merit, there are certain standards and codes to adhere, and when these are violated, knowingly, there are consequences, like being asked to leave. It meant a kind of spiritual death to me — far worse than physical death in many ways because I'd have to live every day with the consequences, knowing the opportunity I had lost.

I felt nauseous and sick to my stomach. At a loss for anything left to do, I fell to my knees and began to sob and beg Prophet not to let this happen, not to let me go. An unknown amount of time passed. I heard Prophet quietly say from across the small, one-room cabin where our class was held, "Lorraine, can you come over to me." It was all I could do to crawl across the floor to him, never once daring to look up. I was not clean in the eyes of God. I had allowed some very negative forces into my life because of earthly desires, desperate for the affections of yet another man I thought I was in love with. I had compromised my values and lost myself. I had chosen man over God, again. A pattern of addiction I had yet to come to terms with.

As God's representative on Earth, Prophet has the authority to cast out such negative forces, evil that overtakes an individual, but until that time I had never seen it done in the seventeen years I had known him. We are all responsible for our actions, and our errors help us learn, sometimes at great expense.

At his feet I sobbed pleading over and over, "I am sorry. I am so sorry." Tears of remorse and sorrow flooded out of me. There was no way I could look up. All remained suspended in time until my intercessor spoke. He asked the small group to quietly sing HU as he placed his hands on my head and prayed. After a while he said to me, "Look up Lorraine." Still low on my knees before him, I summoned the courage to slowly look up. When I did, I beheld the most magnificent sight — eyes filled with the purest love, compassion, and mercy I have ever seen; then he said in the most tender and loving way, "It's okay now. Just don't do it again." Oh the mercy! Glory be to God! I was clean! I had been given another chance. This would not be the end, but rather, the beginning of a deeper level of trust, love, and reverence for God and His Prophet and a renewed commitment to personal responsibility and self-discipline. It would take several years to recover from this and work to regain lost ground, but by the Grace of God I would not have to walk this path back from hell alone.

Prophet would be there to help me every step of the way, as he has been all along.

How did this happen? A year and a half earlier, several months after my divorce from Jeff was final, I again did not give myself any time in between ending and starting a new relationship. I met a man at a work conference. If there was ever an audition in a play for the part of Prince Charming he would have won the role. Not that he was all that physically pleasing — he was just average. It was how he attempted to be "the perfect guy," the ideal I had always sought. He worked overtime at it: romantic dinners, lavish gifts, and loads of attention. I thought, "Wow he does exist." He once bought me a bronze sculpture of a prince-looking figure helping a lady down from a horse. It was over the top and makes me want to gag now, but then I was thrilled with it. What I wasn't aware of was how I was slowly losing myself and selling myself out to be with him. He would be the horseshoe nail in my life that nearly cost me the Kingdom of God. It happened so insidiously, in quiet and hidden ways so not to raise my attention to it at first. Of course now in looking back I see all the signs. It makes me angry, disappointed in myself and ashamed of how I behaved, but it was a necessary lesson I needed on many levels, and for that I am grateful.

I so wanted this fantasy world I had built in my mind to be true, and he did everything he could to keep me blissfully immersed in it. I began ignoring signs and warnings I was given in dreams, awake dreams, and other ways because I didn't want truth. I made those choices to not take heed because I wanted this illusion. It doesn't deserve to be called a relationship really, but I wanted it so badly. I was essentially choosing this outer material world attachment over my inner sacred spiritual marriage to Prophet, which is ultimately the most important to choose over everything in the outer material world — no matter what. I forsook my primary spiritual connection and began to lose the ability to hear Prophet's guidance. And because I stopped listening the consequence was I eventually could not hear his warnings at all. I was too head over heels thinking I had found someone who would finally make me happy. I compromised a lot in many ways to be with this man and lost myself by forsaking that which was so important to me.

But this wasn't just a bad selection in men though; this was far more dangerous. There were negative forces driving this person meant to deliberately steer me away from the path of light and sound. Why? Because when one gets serious about their commitment to God and serving Him as a coworker, being trained and ordained by God's Prophet to become a distributor of God's Love on Earth which has so much darkness in it; well let's just say the other side takes notice. There are many names given to these negative forces in the Bible and other writings, and they are very real. The Tempter's job is to get one pulled off the path home to God, to trip you up, to keep Soul imprisoned in the world of illusion, and not let it know its true nature. It does whatever it can to keep Soul in bondage. It doesn't come as a grotesque figure with horns and a pitch fork, it's far more subtle and devious. It will come disguised as the one thing we are most weak and vulnerable to — our Achilles' heel. The negative side uses passions of the mind such as lust, greed, anger, guilt, fear, vanity, excessive attachment to worldly things, ways of thinking, and people to keep one in spiritual prison. A major part of Prophet's job with me and other students is to gently help us become aware of our main passions of the mind that are holding us back and tripping us up. He teaches us tools to help nourish Soul to get it to wake up and become strong. He frees us by getting Soul so activated and in control of our lives in all areas that we achieve "escape velocity." We break free of the negative forces or gravity that pulls Soul down and keeps us here in prison. Once we are more consistently operating as Soul, we become spiritually free to soar and can more fully enjoy the abundance of our inheritance as children of God. This is the abundance Jesus spoke of that he came to bring (John 10:10). But as long as we are blind to our lower natures, these passions, we are vulnerable to the tricks and traps of the dark side.

There were areas in my life I had made progress, but in the area of relationships with men I was still a mess. The more desperate I became to find the ideal someone, the more in danger I became and without realizing it, I began wanting that more than God. With the choices I made I traded the guidance and protection of Prophet — to a degree. He never left me, but he allowed me my freewill to make these choices and experience the consequences of my actions, as a way of teaching me. Had I listened to his cautions and inner warnings over the year I spent with this person, it might not have had to come to the point it did, but I didn't listen. Spiritually, I was essentially bitten by a venomous snake because I let myself go unprotected. The poison slowly worked its way through my being and began causing my spiritual senses to dim and go numb. I did not have clarity about the situation I was in. I was completely clueless and ignorant to what was happening. In a very real outer confirmation that this was no joke, I discovered multiple nests of poisonous copperhead snakes living in an old retaining wall at my house that runs the length of my driveway up to the front steps. These snakes were hanging out on the stairway going up to my house! I discovered this about a year after being with this guy. I had an expensive teardown and replacement project to get rid of the problem, and all together they removed thirty-three venomous snakes. It is only by God's Grace and protection I or any of my visitors was not bit. About the same time another very expensive item, my car, which should have run another seventy-five to one hundred thousand miles abruptly died and needed to be replaced. The frame underneath rusted out and broke free in a critical joint. My mechanic said it was a miracle the car did not have a serious failure and cause me to flip over and crash while I was driving at highway speeds, which I had done for significant distances before I discovered the problem. Cars and houses in the "Language of the

Divine" often symbolize our inner spiritual life and state of consciousness. Both were telling me I was in grave danger of dying spiritually, and quite possibly dying a physical death too. This would be an expensive lesson on both the inner and outer. If I were listening these would have been awake dreams to warn me, but I had gone deaf. I was no longer moving toward God, I was losing ground I had gained, fast. I was on the road to hell.

After about a year of my unknowing decline toward spiritual death, I invited this man to attend one of Prophet's retreats with me at the retreat center. With immense love and mercy, Prophet chose to put an end to it all that weekend and begin to wake me up from my stupor. It may have appeared as a harsh awakening, but I was so gaga for this guy, so out of tune with Prophet and asleep spiritually he needed a megaphone to get me to hear him and a brick over my head to get my attention. During the retreat Prophet gave me clarity and the ability to once again hear him as a gift of love. In doing so, he gave me a chance to make a conscious choice. Which way did I want to go? Stay on this road or get rid of this guy — completely and totally; not to ever have any dealings with him for I was too susceptible to being bitten again. Once out of my stupor, I was horrified to see what had happened to me of my own doing, and I chose wisely. I chose Prophet and I chose God.

The effects of the evil I allowed into my life were still in me though and required Prophet's intervention to fully cleanse me and get my spiritual senses working once again. He did this in the cabin during Spirit Week the following spring, after things had a chance to settle down and seeing if I would really follow through and leave this guy, which I did. I truly was delivered from evil in the truest sense of the word. Something had to change, or it would just be a matter of time before my earthly desires once again set me up for another fall, but next time, Prophet warned me, he would let me go. If I was that stupid and spiritually immature, then I just wasn't ready for his advanced level of instruction. I heard him and vowed to make a fundamental change.

# 14
# Gift of Abstinence

I stood against the post of the retreat center building talking with Del during a break. It had been a turbulent and exhausting weekend for me, having watched everything come to a head with the guy I had brought to the retreat. This person I brought was asked to leave in the middle of the retreat when his true motivation was revealed through his own words and actions. It was clear to everyone, even me, he was not polarized toward the light but rather the dark forces. I am sure Prophet knew the deal long before this. He allowed things to play out the way they did before putting a stop to it, so I could get the maximum benefit and learning from this, without allowing me or any of the other students to get seriously hurt or impacted spiritually by his being there.

There truly is evil in this world, and while we shouldn't walk around in fear of it those who are naïve to it, like I was back then are at risk and vulnerable to becoming its prey. This is not intended to say I was a victim though. Ignorant or not of the ways of the world, I am still responsible and accountable for my actions. If one is aware evil actively exists in the world, it becomes a form of protection against it. I had a lesson to learn about myself and the world I live in. Knowing there are positive and negative forces actively at work in the world is simply part of growing up and becoming more spiritually mature. It is also a necessary part of living a more abundant life because you cannot ever maintain any sort of real momentum if you keep tripping over the same bad habits and behaviors that cause you problems. Knowing yourself and your weaknesses, where you are at risk and can be tempted, is a hugely important part of protecting yourself against such things. Once you know where you are most vulnerable and the types of situations, environments, or people that contribute to your weakness, then you can make conscious choices to make adjustments or avoid them all together. This is doing our part to be responsible for our own spiritual wellbeing. Another major part is the love and protection Prophet will provide to assist his student, which one often never sees or is aware of but is very real. I know without a doubt Prophet was watching me like a mother hen all through this difficult lesson, making sure I got the full dose of the experience without allowing one drop more than was good and beneficial for me, even though the whole thing scared the daylights out of me once I began to get clarity back. I was actually so frightened I wanted to lock myself in my house and never talk to or be with anyone ever again. But this too was something I would need to work through over the coming months and years, to not be afraid of life or living. These fears lessened over time, but I did struggle with them for a long while.

So on this day as Del and I were talking he said to me maybe it would be a good idea to take a break from dating, give myself some time to clear my head, maybe for two to three years. I listened and agreed for I had been given the very same thought through our inner communication; only I was thinking a good five years. I told Prophet what I was thinking and as the words "for a good five years" came out of my mouth, a part of me said, "What? Are you kidding me? Do you think you can really go five years without dating?" This part of me, the lower part that had largely been running the show up until now, was incredulous I would make such a crazy statement. But I had been scared straight, so to speak, and Soul was able to get a word in edgewise at the moment. I vowed to Prophet and God I would make a fundamental change. I promised I would never allow such a thing to happen again. The real me, Soul, was speaking and starting to put its foot down. Too much was at stake, and with the blessings of clarity and strength I had been given I knew I could do whatever it would take for as long as it took.

And the clock began. My lower self kept track of every month that ticked by as a child counting down to Christmas. "Has it been long enough? Am I ready to date again?" The thought of going five years was almost unthinkable — it felt like forever. There were moments in those first twelve months this promise I made to abstain from dating really felt like a self-imposed death sentence, as if the excitement had gone from life. Eventually that lower part of me got onboard with the plan and quieted down, piping up from time to time requiring me to reaffirm my commitment to this vow. Soul was going to have its way though, and what a blessing it has been! Something that helped me during this time was to focus on doing things for others rather than moping around thinking woe is me. I signed up and trained to be a volunteer at the Children's Hospital in town where I had the opportunity to spend time with some cancer patients and hold infants fighting for their lives when their parents could not be there to give them love. I found great joy in this.

Abstinence is generally thought of as going without something that is wanted or enjoyed. In my case it was the excessive attachment to seeking to be in some form of an "ideal" relationship and gaining fulfillment from it. It wasn't the desire to be with someone that was unhealthy; it was the excessive attachment and blind way I went about searching for it, compromising my core values and losing myself in the process. I abstained from the outer physical activity and asked for strength and help in developing the self-discipline and personal responsibility to be successful. At first I did this through sheer willpower to honor the promise I made to God, but I think God took notice of my commitment to be true to my word and His Grace was upon me through Prophet. What I mean by this is it became less and less of a struggle to do, requiring less and less willpower as the months and years went by. I began to live this vow to abstain not only because of the promise I had made, but because I started to see how good it was for me. Eventually it didn't require willpower and no longer felt like I was giving anything up I wanted or enjoyed. I began to realize I was never really happy living the way I had been living. I no longer wanted that way of life.

My newly emerging lifestyle was becoming more natural and effortless. At the same time it was also creating a sacred space in my life for Prophet to help me. Through many, many inner experiences with God's Light and Sound at retreats, in dreams, and at home in contemplation, I was given healing upon healing, grace upon grace, blessing upon blessing, and they gave me forward momentum. Prophet helped me not just repair the damage done spiritually, but he fortified me, reinforced the weak spots, and helped me come back even stronger. He helped me grow in humility, compassion, patience, strength, and wisdom. Our precious relationship grew in trust and deeper in love. I was more devoted to him than ever before and it has been wondrous! He brought me to higher and higher views of life and gave me a whole new perspective of love; an extraordinary kind of love, different from anything I could ever comprehend before — unconditional, selfless love. He demonstrated this for me in the most profound, magnificent, and sublime ways. I also put tools I was taught, like gratitude, into practice. I focused on what I had, not on what I did not have. There were so many blessings in my life to be grateful for, and this kept my heart open and my spirits high.

This time out from the merry-go-round has been a beautiful time to experience love in so many different ways I had previously not valued or even gave much thought. I never knew anything so splendid and fulfilling could be experienced while one was "alone." But that is part of the treasure I discovered: I may be alone, but I am rarely ever lonely. I knew Prophet was always with me before, but not until I was truly alone with myself, without the distractions and emotional rollercoaster ride relationships had been for me, did I truly get to know how God's Prophet can be there for me in daily life in every challenge, every victory, and in every situation. I have been blessed with a whole new view, finding joy in the smallest parts of creation and the simplest pleasures of life.

One of the simple pleasures in life for me is enjoying a cup of tea. Sometimes after a long bustling day I like to sit and enjoy a hot cup of tea and just be quiet. Even though I know Prophet is there, I don't want to take his presence for granted, so I'll consciously invite him to share a cup of tea with me. There is something beautiful and very special about sitting in silence with someone you love. One particular winter evening as we sat having tea listening to the crackling of the fire, I was feeling especially grateful for its warmth that frigid night. I was also appreciating the gifts of health to cut the wood that was burning, a warm home, the kitty curled up on my lap, knowing who the current Prophet is, and being able to share this time together with him in his inner form. Spontaneously, I began to sing HU. HU is a Love song to God and in singing HU I was expressing my love and saying, "Thank You for all this abundance."

Prophet took me to a place in the inner spiritual worlds that is peaceful, calm, and very still. There was no time and no movement. It just was. It was exquisite! It was like an oasis of tranquility. My whole being smiled and was filled with joy as I listened to the sound of Divine Spirit, the sweet music of the heavens. Its life-giving energy flowed through me. I rested there with Prophet and was nourished and rejuvenated.

A time-out. A deep breath. What once felt like a death sentence became the crucible in which the Holy Fire of God would continue Its works in me. Prophet made ordinary things extra ordinary and began turning everyday occurrences, like this simple cup of tea, into sacred experiences to savor and cherish. I saw that by inviting him into my heart and nurturing our relationship my life was becoming even more blessed — in ways beyond imagination. The true dreams of my heart started to become reality. His love flowed more freely into every aspect of my life, inspiring and uplifting me to greater awareness, love, and abundance.

# 15

# Oasis of Tranquility

*"Live in Balance and Harmony"* is a quote from Del printed on Guidance for a Better Life T-shirts. It is more than just a quote though; it embodies the very heart of what he teaches. I think it is also a prayer he holds in his heart for us, his beloved students. It is an easy phrase to say, but it has taken me years to understand and lifetimes, literally lifetimes, to try to master. The spiritual tools and ways of the Divine that Del has been teaching me since first coming to his retreat center were there to enable me to walk through life this way, to align myself and my life with God's ways and be right with Him. In time, abundance and joy began to flourish in my life and I grew in ability to find and maintain my own balance, and walk in harmony with Divine Spirit as my true self, Soul.

One of these skills that made a real difference in the quality of my life was learning to make time every day for quiet contemplation and prayer. I dedicate this time to be with the Divine, express my love and gratitude, gain insights, or sing HU, a song of love and thanks to God. This became the cornerstone of my day and consecrated my thoughts, actions, and intentions. These precious minutes are like finding an oasis of tranquility in the midst of chaos and the rush of daily life, responsibilities, or burdens carried. It is an oasis of Living Water I am immersed in that nourishes me. It sustains me throughout the day, so when life is happening all around I can operate from a higher point of view, see clearer, listen deeper, keep my heart open, be more discerning and make better decisions, have patience, show compassion, and give love.

Making this sacred time for prayer and communication with God really turned the tide, especially in taking time *to listen* to Him. This, and continuing to build my Divine relationship with Prophet, made all the difference. It is how I learned to find the oasis of tranquility within me and live in balance and harmony. I went from being able to experience this for a short time during a retreat, to being able to find it during contemplation time, to integrating it more and more into daily life, aspiring to live every day in this way. The sacred gift of time to experience life in a new way on my own helped me greatly in moving toward this goal.

# 16

# A Country Girl After All

I can recall reading books in my adult life about individuals and families moving from the city to homestead in the wilderness somewhere, and I marveled at how they lived. One family with two small children lived fourteen months in a canvas, MASH-style tent through the winter in interior Alaska, having to cut and burn a cord of wood each day to keep warm. Another family with eight children built a home on a lake above the Arctic Circle sixty miles off the nearest road; and a single woman hacked out her life in a densely forested area of British Columbia, building her own log cabin and baking bread each day over an open fire while fending off grizzly bears. Something about their stories captivated me and drew me to travel a half dozen times or so to see these wild areas for myself, even meeting and staying with one of these ladies I read about. But anything of the sort for me seemed to be just a fantasy. I was born and lived most of my life in cities, my job was located in a major city, and I had zero experience in the skills necessary for homesteading and living a sustainable life: gardening, carpentry, woodcutting, hunting, and raising animals for food. One could always dream though...

The Blue Ridge Mountains of Virginia, while not the raw and harsh wilderness of some of the places I read about and visited, were in many ways much more inviting and inspiring to me. While attending retreats over the years at Guidance for a Better Life, I fell in love with the area of Virginia where the retreat center is located, and it came to feel like home to me. I dreamed of owning a little patch of land and maybe having a little cabin of my own there someday. Maybe not going full-bore into homesteading, but even integrating a few aspects of a more self-sufficient, sustainable life in the mountains would quench my thirst for the kind of life that beckoned me. To my rational mind it was a near impossibility though, at least until after I retired and was not so tethered to my city-based life and location-specific profession. I never stopped dreaming even though I did not know how, or if, this would ever occur. One day I thought, "Well let me just look at some properties and see what is available." I was led to the perfect real estate agent who searched with me for about nine months looking for the right place. As she got to know me she began to recommend places I would not have thought to look at, and one day she called and said she really wanted me to look at this one place. It was a much larger piece of land and more home than I had been thinking of, but she felt it was something I might like. As I drove up the long, steep driveway to the house I became emotional because she was right. It was perfect. I met the lovely elderly couple who built the place, and as I toured the property, in spite of being overwhelmed thinking, "No way — this is too much," it started to feel comfortable, like this could become home. Things worked out and I was able to buy the home. I enjoyed it as a vacation place, coming down a couple weekends a month, resisting the drive back to Washington D.C on Sunday evenings, sometimes convincing myself I could make the three-hour drive in on Monday morning, trying to stretch my time there. My plan was to retire there in about fifteen years, but God had a different plan. As I look back, I see that for years God was working miracle after miracle, arranging circumstances, setting things up, and presenting opportunities that would not just make my dream come true, but His dream for me come true — which blew mine out of the water! It was more than I could ever dare to imagine for myself.

One Sunday while driving back to D.C. I noticed a new building going up on the north side of Charlottesville, and it happened to be with the same agency I worked for. "Wow," I thought, "Wouldn't it be great if I could work from down here?" as far-fetched as that sounded to me at the time for a number of reasons. God knew the dreams in my heart long before I could ever express them, and He had been at work for years lining things up to make this happen, long before I ever noticed. Within two years of verbalizing it, several incredible "coincidences" occurred that landed me a job there. These were not coincidences though; looking back I see the Hand of God was at work clearing a path for me to live my dream. One of the "coincidences" was an act of the United States Congress. In an effort to consolidate infrastructure and reduce overhead costs, Congress directed a move of certain job functions down to the Charlottesville area which would require someone in my line of work. Interestingly, I had gained some of these skills and professional contacts through the deployment to Afghanistan several years earlier. The move would come at a cost though to the continued successful upward trajectory of my career. Moving away from Washington also meant being further away from headquarters and the senior-most positions I was being prepared for and on track to hold one day. I knew I was not only forfeiting any further promotion, salary, or grade increase, but I would also have to take a ten percent cut in pay as salaries are based, in part, on location. It meant some soul-searching and asking myself if this move was what I really wanted. I knew the demands and personal costs on my life as it currently was, and I had a taste of what life could be like in the mountains from just being there on weekends; I always found it difficult to leave. To my colleagues and my logical mind this was career suicide — who would do such a thing? But my heart was being drawn forward to a new life. There was a bold excitement I felt in following it. I did not know what lay ahead, but I knew I had to go. So against society's suggested road to "success," I chose a different path. Success is a personally defined idea based on one's priorities. The classes and retreats I had taken helped me be clear on what these were. My priorities had changed a great deal since moving to Washington D.C. seventeen years earlier. With a little courage to follow my heart, I could better align my life with them and decide how much energy and focus I put on doing different things. What freedom! There is great freedom in making conscious choices and exercising the free will God has given us! With this decision there came a peace into my life I can only describe as that moment of stillness that occurs at the end of a long deep breath and exhale — only longer.

This move allowed me to live in the mountains just six miles as the crow flies from Guidance for a Better Life and my beloved spiritual guide and teacher, Del. I could now live full-time in a slice of heaven. I was home! Living on a beautiful piece of land I had lots of opportunity to experiment and develop the skills I was inspired by in others' life stories. Every step of the way I felt Divine Spirit guiding me to the right people, books, and online information sources, and more importantly, giving me the courage to jump right in and try. The more I tried and learned, the more confidence I gained. The more confidence I gained, the less insecure I felt. As I grew more secure and confident in my own abilities, the over-reliance on others to fulfill what I could do for myself faded. That is not to say I did not accept help and went to the other extreme, but I just wasn't depending on someone to take care of me and my needs all the time, and it felt good. I liked being able to stand on my own and be more self-sufficient. I felt less needy overall, and I gained more insight into how I used to view relationships. Part of my reason for selecting and being with the people I was with in the past was that they could do things I thought I could not. I needed them to be able to get by in life whether it was finances, yard work, home repairs, plowing the driveway when it snowed, or any number of other responsibilities. They filled the "something" I didn't think I could do for myself. Life on my own gave me a chance to see I was capable of much more than I thought. And what I could not do for myself, I could trust myself to know how to go about hiring or finding someone to help me get it done.

Living there also allowed me to spread my wings and learn some other skills like hunting deer. Thanks to all those who post videos on YouTube and lots and lots of inner instruction on what to do from Prophet, I killed my first deer the first fall after moving to my place, albeit in a skirt one morning as I was going off to work. After changing clothes, I went out to prepare the deer for skinning and processing. I cannot describe the humility and awe I felt crouched on the ground going through the steps necessary if one is to have fresh, healthy meat to eat. Physically I went through the tasks at hand, but emotionally and spiritually I was awestruck. What a miracle of creation God made in this beautiful creature. The way it moves with such grace and beauty, the intricacies of the design of the deer's body and its organs, combined with its keen senses and gentle ways, are incredible. I felt responsible not to waste one ounce of meat, leaving the innards I couldn't use as a meal for the wildlife that consumed them within a few short hours. Remembering my first meal of fresh venison still brings tears to my eyes for so many reasons I can hardly explain, and it is with deep appreciation and love I credit God's Holy Spirit working in my life that allowed me such an amazing experience. I believe God made it so easy for me to get this deer to help me build confidence that I could do this, just as He did all those years ago in the tracking class, when I never thought I would ever want to track anything to hunt it. It wasn't the cruel and mean act I had mistakenly judged it to be. It felt sacred and created a deeper respect for and bond with the magnificent creation that surrounded me. I understood at a deeper level than ever we can trust God to provide for all of our needs.

A couple summers later, I had a strong desire to build a chicken coop and start keeping chickens. I had never done anything like carpentry or woodworking before and had very little to no experience with the tools and materials I would need for the job. I was quite wary at first and afraid of power tools and saws. I was not even sure of the design I wanted. One day while out shopping I saw very cute (very expensive) pre-made chicken coops for sale. For a moment I was tempted to buy one and just skip right to raising the chickens, but I heard Prophet's voice inside remind me how I had wanted to learn to build things. He reassured me we could do this. The inner Prophet was helping me on this project ... while out shopping, during quiet contemplation time, and in dreams. He helped me with the design and led me to various books and resources that gave me a basic understanding of what I needed to do to build the foundation, construct the window frames, and put up the siding and roofing. He gave me confidence to try out new features we dreamed up and change things along the way that weren't working. He also helped me find a wonderful source for mature chickens that would be laying right away in a nearby town I could bring home to the new coop. I discovered I love chickens! Going out to the chicken coop in the mornings and evenings brings me such joy. I eagerly await the greeting I receive and laugh with all the clucking and chatter coming from "the girls," which is what I call my hens. I talk to them, asking how their day went and thank them for the beautiful eggs they laid. Eggs are such a miracle to me. They inspire awe and appreciation of God's perfection every time I collect them. The coop isn't very big and probably not all that impressive to someone who knows how to build things, but for me it is grand. When I go outside and see it I am filled with gratitude and appreciation for all the help I had in accomplishing this project and realizing more of my dream.

Most days I spend quiet moments in prayer before work. Nestled up in the mountains I may read from scripture and reflect on the passages, letting the precious words settle deeper into my heart as they continue to nourish me through the day. Sometimes I sing HU. Other times I just sit quietly in Prophet's presence. I will often sit in a chair in the great room looking out of the large windows that frame a serene panorama of trees, valley, and mountains.

God's breathtaking artistry! There are mornings I pinch myself to be living in such a beautiful place. I can hardly believe this is my life now. To be able to provide my own meat and eggs, grow fresh vegetables, have plenty of wood to heat my home, the means to prepare for being snowbound in winter, and think creatively to solve different problems and situations that arise; I found this lifestyle suits me much more than city life. God knew this. He knew the dreams I was holding in my heart and made it a reality, helping me gradually overcome fears that would have limited my ability to live this lifestyle. I was no longer afraid of the dark as I was when I first arrived at Del's retreat center, or to be alone by myself. I overcame my fear of guns, chainsaws, or anything else with a motor and sharp parts that might hurt me. I was confident in my ability to learn new things, and I began to trust myself in certain areas. I surrendered to God and stayed open to inner guidance from His Holy Spirit. I embraced the opportunities He presented and did my part. I witnessed miracle upon miracle while watching my dreams come true. My little brother was right. His words about me all those years ago were prophetic. It turns out I am a country girl after all.

# 17

# Take the Cure Leave the Label

~~~~

The thing about being on your own is that you have the opportunity to be alone with yourself, a lot. With the distraction of the relationship merry-go-round I was on gone, all there was now was me. I was no longer spending energy running away from who I was or afraid to be alone with my own thoughts and feelings. I wanted to see what would unfold if I truly allowed myself to just be, to live a little more simply, and not feel like I had to fill every moment with someone or rushing off to some activity. I made a conscious choice not to fill up all my free time with hobbies, trips, and activities for awhile. These are not bad things and are very healthy to have, in balance, but they can also be used to fill the void left from dropping one type of distraction with yet another. I felt what was best for me at this time in my life was to give myself the gift of space, solitude, and self-reflection. It was a very special time, and I was blessed with the opportunity to look within and take a peak under that carpet where I had swept so many things.

Who was I really? I was not very comfortable with who I was. I felt lacking in some way and like I had to prove myself to be accepted or loved. I began to see some things I never wanted to look at before. There were negative habits and behaviors I had picked up in life, like road dirt on the windshield of a beautiful sports car. These defilements or passions of the mind were things I felt the effects of but was largely blind to otherwise. Since I could not see them clearly, I kept stumbling into them and tripping over them not knowing why. This made me angry at myself, made me feel defective, and stole joy from life. These negative traits and tendencies made it difficult to operate as my true self, Soul. They estranged me from the boundless splendor of my true nature.

I was guided to seek professional help and began seeing a mental health specialist. At first I felt weak conceding I had a problem, but I was shown that was not true — it takes courage and strength to seek help and be willing to change. The therapist I saw was a wonderfully compassionate and skilled clinician who helped me see ways I used delusion and self-deception as a means of escape from certain situations. What was I escaping from though? She and I looked at my early years. It wasn't easy to face, but I realized I had unresolved situations from childhood and I needed help working through them. Until now I only thought of the positive things and the happy times we shared as a family, but that wasn't the whole story. I needed to look at and accept the whole truth, not just the bus trips and Christmas mornings. I love my family very much and I am thankful to my parents for all they have done; they gave so much in raising their children. I felt I was being ungrateful and disloyal to them by admitting there were serious issues with the environment in which I was raised. That wasn't true though, I was and still am very grateful for all they did. In a strange way I was relieved and so thankful once we finally started looking back.

I received help both on the inner and outer from Prophet, and with the strength, clarity, and encouragement he brought me I could finally face what I previously could not. I began to see there were unacknowledged parts of me and my life that hurt every relationship I tried to have. This helped me begin to understand the roots of the unhealthy ways I sought love and the illusions I created around it. Going back, I found memories of events and situations that were painful, overwhelming, disturbing, and frightening to me. At an early age, as a means of coping, I began censoring these unpleasant parts and dissociated from them, leaving a void of disconnectedness and numbness in its place. To break through the numbness I developed a tendency toward exaggerated behavior and gestures in order to feel or express something when it was important to me.

For the nine months I spent in counseling I invited Prophet into each weekly session and asked him to guide me in my effort to get well. I felt him working through my therapist and guiding our meetings. He brought deeper insights to what was discussed in sessions through my dreams. He gave me additional clarity through my daily contemplations and reflections on scripture, always leading me to just the right passages and books to read. God's Love was penetrating the numbness I held at my core. What was hidden was revealed: fears and pains of abandonment, not feeling safe and secure, lack of inherent self-worth, guilt, and shame. These were not intentionally put on me by anyone, just stuff I felt and interpreted from situations and circumstances as they were. These things I had been carrying, unknowingly, were causing me pain and acting as blockages to God's Love. I was shown that some of these roots even extended back to a previous lifetime and was helped to offload this baggage and begin to heal.

I acknowledged and took responsibility for poor decisions I had made and the self-destructive attitudes and behaviors I developed, especially when it came to relationships with men. In search of love, I had become addicted to it. I was in love with the "idea," the "illusion" of love, and this resulted in a lifelong pattern of unhealthy relationships.

After four years of abstaining from intimate relationships and dating, I was sufficiently clean of the intoxicating effects that being with someone had on me, and the professional help I now sought could be effective. I clearly saw these old ways of being and they no longer had any place in my life. In preparing for a session one day, I realized I had been in a continuous string of relationships in one form or another for thirty-five years straight, with the exception of a few months here or there, with nineteen different people. The therapist actually had a clinical diagnosis for this condition called

"Love Addiction." It operates as any other addiction does taking an unhealthy place in one's life, making "that thing" more in control of one's life rather than the individual. Taking a long time-out from dating and relationships was like getting sober for an alcoholic. This was an act inspired by God because He knew His gift of abstinence was what I needed to begin to get well. He wasn't asking me to go without love though, just the opposite. He more than made up for not having another person in my life to give and receive love from. He rained His Love down upon me in countless ways I never thought could be so filled with awe and splendor. He showered me with love every way imaginable: through His creation, through other Souls, and even through my chickens, rabbits, and lovable sweet kitty, Sunshine. He filled me and healed my aching heart. I was so well cared for all through this time, I never ever was left feeling as if I lacked anything. He opened my eyes to a whole new and glorious view of love, true love, His Love. A love that is like no other.

One that was more realistic, positive, and healthy.

Knowing this time in therapy was a gift from God, I fully embraced what was being offered. I devoured the books and exercises the therapist prescribed, but labeling myself as those things she diagnosed did not feel right. The only label I want on me is "Soul" a child of God. That isn't to deny the reality of the dynamics that were at work in my life, or the fact that there may be days when I get triggered by something and have a desire to fall back into one of these old habits, but accepting the label she diagnosed the condition to be felt like overly subscribing to it; like I was putting a stamp on my forehead and permanently identifying with that lower part of my nature. The lower self does have its issues and hang-ups, but I do not want that to be my focus. I aspire to operate more as my true self, the Divine eternal being I am, Soul. That is where I want my focus and energy to be. It is a delicate balance because while I do not want to deny challenges I face, given the tendencies and old habits that are there, I do not want to feed them or make them stronger by overly identifying with them either.

Visualizing where I want to be and what I aspire to is more important to me than looking backwards. Without Prophet I do not think this would be possible, but with the extra ordinary help that comes with knowing him and using the spiritual tools he has taught me, it is very possible; for nothing is impossible with God. I am a testament to this because for more than five years now I have been walking in greater balance and harmony, specifically in this area of my life, because of Him. With His help these negative things no longer have the same control over my life as they did before because of the cumulative blessings and direct experiences in the Light and Sound of God. He has uplifted me and given me a whole new view of life, a different state of consciousness. I see more clearly, hear inner guidance more clearly, and have tools to help me regroup and get back on track when I have an off day. Overall, I have been making more conscious choices that are good for me. Through the Grace, Love, and blessings of God, and Prophet's continued help, the process of healing, learning, and growing from this has brought more abundance to my life.

My parents did the best they knew how to do and were dealing with their own challenges, so there is no blame being ascribed here. I came into this life with certain "weak spots" in my own character and with unresolved issues from past lifetimes. The conditions of my childhood just brought them to the surface, so I could continue to learn and grow in these areas in this life. From this multiple-lifetime higher view of Soul, everything was as it needed to be. It was all perfect. Looking under the carpet was an important first step. Being willing to acknowledge what was there and accept the truth of things as they were, made it possible to receive the healings and be released from it all. Truth really does have the power to set one free!

# 18

# Gift of a Special Mirror

During a retreat I took early on in the same time I was in therapy, Del brought a group of his students spiritually to visit a temple in one of God's inner Heavens. As we began, he asked us to think of something we were grateful for — what first came to mind was Prophet himself. I was grateful to be his student and for the bond of love we share that is the center of my life. This opened my heart as we sang HU, a love song to God.

He took us in our Soul bodies to the temple's doorway. We were welcomed by a glorious Being in a white robe and were invited into his sacred place. After several experiences in this ancient and Holy place of God I received a gift. The gift was a mirror, and although I did not look into it yet, I knew I had been given something valuable that would help me. We sang HU once again as we came back from the visit into our physical bodies. It felt as if we had travelled down within a brilliant-white beam of light. Gradually my consciousness shifted back to my physical body. The spiritual mirror I received came down with me through the beam of God's Light. As we continued to sing HU, I spiritually went to my knees thankful for being in the presence of such sacredness. I could have sung that love song to God forever. Gratitude, love, and appreciation flowed forth from me like a fountain. I was so happy expressing what was in my heart. In doing so, I felt it satisfy a deep need I had inside me to draw close to God.

My eyes still closed, I spent quiet time with the inner Prophet. He suggested I look into the mirror now. As I did, I saw a flash of white light and felt myself expanding and rising. My awareness was enlarged and uplifted. I sensed God's sacred Light shining on areas of my life where I had been hiding from truth. I had a knowingness this was the beginning of a process that would continue. This gift took the inner visual form of a mirror, but it was really a blessing from God. Through God's Prophet, this blessing would continue to show me truth and bring clarity and understanding. It would bring me strength, healing, and peace. I received a lot of help from Prophet during this retreat, very directly and intensely at times.

A little while after this experience, I was sitting quietly one evening with my focus on the inner Prophet after singing HU. I saw an image of the mirror I had been given. Instead of having me look into it, this time Prophet placed it into my heart to reflect the beauty within. With the sacred mirror forever inside me now, he reminded me of who I really am, Soul. He showed me the unique God-given qualities I am made of, reconnecting me with them and my true nature. I began to weep at the beauty of what I felt in that moment as I saw the beautiful child of God I am, safe and protected in my Heavenly Father's Hands, and dearly, dearly loved. This, and the countless other blessings bestowed upon me during this special time, made it possible to move forward, more free and more Me than ever before.

# 19

# Past-Life Healing Through a Dream

◦⌒◦≈◦⌒◦

About halfway through my time in counseling Prophet gave me a dream that was part of a multi-year process of healing from a past-life that was related to some of the same challenges I faced in this life. I dreamt I was in my house. It was a multi-storied bright, sunny, and open space. Suddenly I found myself in a different part of the house I did not remember being there, or I had not been in for a long while and had forgotten about. It was on a lower level, perhaps a first floor or basement. It was a separate structure but was attached to my house and shared a common wall. I briefly caught a glimpse of this from the exterior then was back inside. This older attached section was in very bad shape.

When first walking around the large rooms of this older part of the house, it looked as if it might have potential. I thought to myself, maybe I could fix it up and rent it out. Then I looked up and saw the ceilings; they were near collapsing. I noticed the floors; they were torn up and debris was everywhere. It looked as if no one had lived there for awhile, with just a few remnants of former life there. It was so bad all I could think was how expensive it was going to be to fix all this. It would probably require a home equity loan, which I didn't really want to do. It needed to be dealt with right away though, because it was a hazard. I was even afraid being in there because it was so unsafe. I was also concerned about the way it was attached onto the nice, well-built home I presently lived in. I did not want this old section to cause it to collapse or become structurally damaged.

Then something very cool happened: I woke up while still in the dream and became conscious. This has only happened to me once or twice before that I can recall. At first

I was relieved I was in a dream and not in any immediate danger. Then, since I was not in my physical body and therefore not constrained by the body's physical limitations, I started trying things I may not have done otherwise, like putting my fists through the wall and jumping up high enough to go through the ceiling and punch into it. I was covered in dust and plaster board, but knowing it would not collapse on me physically gave me a sense of freedom and boldness to try such things. I realized this dilapidated structure was beyond repair and had to be demolished. I think this was my way of getting things started. I was very concerned when I awoke however, because houses often represent one's state of consciousness when they show up in dreams. Prophet was trying to get my attention to help me, so I asked him for help in understanding the dream he blessed me with.

After a few contemplations and looking at it from different perspectives he helped me see some pearls contained in the dream. I was excessively attached to something from the past and it was negatively impacting this life. Perhaps this was not in an overt or easily noticeable way but in a fundamental (structural) way. The attachment to a past lifetime was symbolized by the section of house I had not been in for a long time. The sunlit, multi-storied part of the home I currently lived in was positive, but the older attached section was bad off and potentially hazardous. The common wall between the older and newer section suggested that in addition to it being something I had a hard time letting go of, there was also an attempt to keep it compartmentalized and isolated or unacknowledged. Trying to ignore it or pretend it wasn't there didn't make it go away. It was hurting my spiritual growth and limiting the freedom, joy, and abundance in my present life because trying to "wall-off" this section was really trying to close my heart to it, and a closed heart to one thing also closes it to other things, including God's Love and blessings.

This information was not totally new to me, as months prior to this Prophet had taken me back to a lifetime in the past that was probably the root of the issue. There was a relationship with someone I cared for and loved very deeply that did not work out as I had wished and I never accepted the outcome or properly dealt with or let go of the disappointment, hurt, and pain that resulted from it. I think many of my lessons in living from my current life in the relationship area are a result of my not having honestly and constructively dealt with the situation from the past and faced things as they were. Maybe because the truth was too much for me to face. Perhaps this was where my tendency of retreating to a world of delusion and fantasy as a way of coping originated. I am not completely sure of this piece, but it does seem plausible. Eventually the unresolved issues we try to ignore or sweep under the carpet will need to be dealt with when we are ready, even if it takes us many, many lifetimes to become strong enough to hit it head on. This is a gift of love, to be able to wait to work on the more difficult challenges and lessons of our personal "spiritual syllabus" until we are strong enough and positioned for success. The only reason I became strong enough in this lifetime to work through this is because I met God's Prophet, and he patiently worked with me for twenty years until I was ready. While it is true just one meeting with God's Prophet can dramatically change one's life for the better, something of this delicate and complex nature cannot be done all at once, not because he is unable to do it, but because it would be too much on someone to try and fix all at once. In Prophet's perfect loving way, he was gently raising and expanding my awareness of the situation, conditioning me little by little at a rate I could handle without it being too much or putting me out of balance. All the while I was being held, loved, and protected in the Hand of God.

What was significant about this dream was how clearly I saw the situation and understood. The dream spoke to me as Soul in my native language more directly and clearly than any words or mental dialogue could have conveyed while awake and without emotions clouding things. What was also very significant was that I woke up in the dream, and with the boldness and confidence of Soul I began to take an active part in taking down the old structure. It was a turning point in both understanding and acceptance of truth given to me by Prophet. I was ready to acknowledge it for what it was, let go of what was holding me back, and move forward.

While driving to work one morning a few weeks after having this dream, I saw a truck with the words "Precision Remodelers" written on the back. This awake dream caught my attention and I knew it was a message for me. It reminded me of the house dream, and how I was concerned in the dream about how to get rid of the old rundown structure without damaging the nice part of the house. I could certainly use a "precision remodeler." I perceived a blessing and inner healing was taking place. Through this entire process that began earlier with the initial past-life Soul travel experience and even before then by conditioning and preparing me, Prophet's precision and expertise was safely helping me dismantle the wall in my heart and attachments to the past I had been holding, without doing damage. He has made it so the love and cherished memories from that time, of which there were many, could flow forward into the present without the negative baggage; that has been let go and replaced with Divine love.

From this I feel my heart was remodeled and upgraded in the sense I can feel and appreciate love in new and deeper ways in many areas. I notice it in a more honest, loving relationship with Prophet, deeper trust, and more precise inner communication with him. I notice it in more genuine and intimate connections and exchanges with friends and family. I have also noticed more Soul-to-Soul interactions with others I meet throughout the day. I even notice it in a deeper savoring, wonder, and appreciation for nature, and in those special little moments when I experience God's Love through the world around me. It is difficult to put into words, but it feels as if a shadow, one I did not even know had cast itself over my already blessed and abundant life has been removed. The numbness and need to withdraw and escape fading into the mists. I am beginning to see richness, color, and depth of life and love I have not experienced before.

God wants the best for His children, and He does not want us to settle for anything less than true happiness and love. He knows I would like to share a uniquely special love with someone someday, but I was going about it all wrong. I know in His time and by following His way it will come. My life, symbolized in the dream by the bright sunny house, was already a very nice house — a beautiful life filled with many blessings. Through this healing process it is becoming even more beautiful, more joyful, more love-filled, and more abundant. It is sometimes hard to imagine, but there truly is always more, to include clearing up old issues that may still be holding us back today. With God and His Prophet there isn't anything that cannot be fixed, even a broken heart.

# 20

# Oh My Gosh — Love!

About a year after this healing dream, I had a sacred experience under Prophet's loving guidance during a retreat that could easily be the highlight of a lifetime. It is one I will never forget. It held great significance and helped me gain a greater capacity to love. It occurred during the third retreat of the five-part "Keys to Spiritual Freedom" study series, "Building Divine Relationships." In this particular retreat Del was focusing on helping us develop and strengthen our relationship with the Divine. Divine is a general term he uses that is inclusive of the aspects of God: His Holy Spirit, also known as the Light and Sound of God or Holy Ghost, the inner and outer forms of God's Prophet, and Soul, which is also Divine by its nature.

We started our journey to the inner Heavens singing HU, a love song to God.

Prophet asked us to think of something we were grateful for specifically from that day, then to ask for an experience of some type that would help us build our relationship with the Divine, and promise to be receptive to whatever blessings were given. I was grateful for something that happened early in the day at home, and then my thoughts just flowed from one moment to the next. Without intending to do so, I ended up going through my day step by step, and saw God's Hand in everything I did, feeling so much gratitude, awe, and deep appreciation for it all. An amazing experience followed. When our inner spiritual journey ended and I came back into my physical body, it took me a while to take it all in. I had a hard time forming words to describe what had happened. What I experienced was so far beyond words and mental concepts, but I did my best to capture the moment. In my journal I wrote:

> "Oh my gosh — LOVE. My heart is just bursting and overflowing with love. It began in my heart, love

pouring out so strong fueled by the gratitude I felt every step of my day — I couldn't just stop at one thing. The love flowed out of me to You Dear God, but it was unlike anything I had ever felt before. A kind of dam broke, a wall or resistance of some type was cleared by Your Grace and love poured out of me. It felt strong, beautiful, and uplifting. Your Divine Spirit beckoned me closer with Its heavenly music, eventually engulfing me into the sound. I felt love, indistinguishable now whether coming out of me to You Lord, or from You to me. It was our love, the love of our relationship. I may have experienced this in a very real way before, but perhaps I am feeling it in a more true sense tonight as whatever hurts or pains I had numbed myself to have been healed, and the protective walls I had built around my heart crumbled in the light of Your security, comfort, and magnificent Love. I cried and cried the *most beautiful tears I have ever felt. It was almost hard to breathe because the feeling of awe from the beauty took my breath away. As I write, even now, the tears keep flowing. "RAPTURE" is the word that is in my heart. This love I feel is incredible! It has been there, but not like this. The love in me has been strong and very much there, building all these years, but now it is flowing, and I can feel it more than ever tonight. Oh my gosh — the tears just keep coming. It is amazing. Thank You!!!"*

This incredible experience took me by surprise. It showed me the depth of the love I had for God that was already there, and then took me even farther initiated by the gratitude and appreciation I felt for all the ways God showed me His Love in just that one day alone... so many ways, big and seemingly small — though there is nothing "small" when it comes to God's Love. Just a drop of it can move mountains. I know to my core I love God and have felt it. I know God and His Prophet love me, and I have felt and experienced this love in many beautiful ways, and yet the degree and intensity of what I felt in this experience knocked my socks off. There truly is always more... wow! It is not random of course. I saw a seamless progression over time from retreat to home to retreat, and a continuous flow of God's Grace and Love: truth, insights, healings, direct experiences with the light and sound, and interaction with different aspects of the Divine. I have been especially blessed with added clarity, strength, and purification by being in Prophet's presence at retreats like this one and at home with his inner form. My heart remains full with gratitude, appreciation, and humbled awe for the new life and richer experiences of love that include greater love for God, for Prophet, for others, and even for myself. Love that was always there that only needed to be unchained, set free, and allowed to soar!

# 21

# To Soar Like an Eagle

Del always seems to be looking for opportunities to help us experience more of our true selves as Soul. He knows every chance to do so is really good for us because it nourishes and strengthens the eternal, true nature in us. It is part of how he frees one under his care. As a God-ordained Prophet this is part of his job and one of the many gifts he is authorized to give. He gradually and gently helps his students get to know themselves as the Divine spiritual beings they are. On one particular day I was blessed to experience the exhilarating freedom of being unchained from the confines of my physical body and its entrapments and limitations.

Prophet asked us to think of something we were grateful for as a way of opening our hearts. I thought of my pet chickens and rabbits that bring joy and love to my life. This brought a big smile to my heart as we sang HU, a love song to God. He then invited us to follow him up through the top of the room we were in, pointing out that in the spiritual worlds, walls and physical structures are not barriers to Soul, which is made of God's Light and Sound. I left my outer body sitting in the chair as I rose up to the ceiling with Prophet in our light bodies. The roof of the building just seemed to melt away as we passed through without effort. Looking down I could see the pond, the retreat center, Del and Lynne's house, and its lights.

Prophet suggested we think of our favorite bird, and I immediately thought of an eagle. I found myself soaring high above the trees and mountains. My large eagle wings moving in deep, slow, strong motions propelled me through the air. I maneuvered unencumbered by the limitations of my "earth suit" or the laws of the physical world. I felt free! I was tasting my Divine nature and the boundlessness of Soul. My vision was excellent. I could see even the smallest of details on the ground and watched various critters scurry in the grasses below. As a way of reassuring us we were still our individual selves, even though we were out of the body, Prophet asked us to think of someone we loved. I thought of him, as our love connection is so precious and close to my heart. Together we soared up the valley and I saw Vision Rock, an outcropping of large rocks on retreat center property that has a magnificent view. It is a special place to us students. I remembered sitting on those rocks watching birds soar by or hearing jet planes roaring overhead, wondering what that might feel like. Now I had an idea, but this experience was not just a joy ride to me. It felt sacred and purposeful. It also had qualities of peace, calm, assuredness, and strength that came from somewhere deep within. Just then, Prophet said, "Do not go too far, stay close to the retreat center property." I think he may have been talking to me. I was having such a great time savoring the freedom and exploring in this way I may have gone a little further than he wanted, so I circled back and made sure I stayed close. When it was time to return from our adventure we were asked to gather as a group and circle the retreat center's pond. I still recognized other students in the retreat even though they appeared as bodies of light. Once we were all there Prophet gently and carefully guided us back down into the building and into our "earth suits."

We are so much more than our physical bodies. We are Soul first that has a body. What a profound and life-changing perspective! For those of us blessed with this experience or ones like it, this statement is not just a mental concept or even a belief. It is reality. Prophet arranged these types of experiences for us so we may gain first-hand knowledge of the truth in this statement and activate the qualities of our true Self. With him in my heart and by my side I was beginning to soar as a spiritual eagle into a glorious reality. I was coming to know this reality more regularly now, claiming my Divinity and living it on a more regular basis. That reality is the reality of Soul.

# 22

# Heaven on Earth

I stood on the steps of God's Temple with Prophet as the other Souls in our group arrived. We had been invited here to visit this sacred temple known as the House of Liberation. We travelled here in our Soul bodies safely escorted by Prophet and were met by the temple's guardian. This was a rare opportunity we had been given to have individualized learning experiences that would nourish, cleanse, and fortify us, and aid in our spiritual growth.

The temple guardian, Prophet, and I walked inside and without a word being exchanged went directly to the beam of God's Light and Sound in the center of the room that seemed to be the very heart and life of the temple itself. I could hear crackling and popping sounds of the dynamic life-giving energy of the beam, its sound loud in my ears. It did not appear as the solid beam of light I had seen before but as large white shimmering sheets of light that had texture. We went into it and the three of us stood inside this beam of Light and Sound of God. I noticed our Soul bodies we wore in these inner worlds were made of the same light and sound as the beam. Made in God's image — this phrase from the Bible took on a deeper meaning to me now. Inside the beam there was stillness and timelessness. The only word that could describe what I felt was "complete." I was complete. In His Light and Sound, God's Essence, there was nothing I lacked. Everything I could ever want or need was right there.

Just then I became aware of being both inside the beam in the temple and also sitting in my chair back at the retreat center. A long shaft of white light from the beam connected me with my Soul body inside the temple with me in my physical body that sat in the chair, the light coming straight into my heart. It felt as if a solid connection of God's Light and Love was made between these two aspects of me. I felt something was being downloaded through this light and was integrating into my physical being. There came a sense of continuity, oneness, and sameness between Soul that was still in Heaven, the physical part of me that was on Earth, and the Light of God that connected us.

A shower of golden light then cleansed and nourished me. I asked for anything that might still be holding me back in life to be let go. I cupped my hands and drank of this golden spiritual water of love as it poured over me and bathed me. I was so filled with love and appreciation for these gifts from Prophet I literally danced in joy.

Soul as created by God is complete, but we are not always conscious of it down here in the physical. Often we search for things outside of us to make us feel whole, secure, or good enough. We forget our true nature, which is one reason God sends His Prophets. Del helped me remember. Through many experiences such as this one, he activated the dormant qualities of Soul. It is an ongoing process of coming to know myself better by recognizing and manifesting these Divine qualities in my life. The completeness I experienced inside the beam, feeling I had everything I could ever want or need, does not mean I shun earthly comforts and pleasures or no longer welcome the blessings of family, friends, or material wealth. It just means I do not *need* those things to make me feel whole. It is so freeing to no longer need others to make me feel good about myself, find self-esteem and self-worth, or to fill something I perceive to be lacking in me. I am free to appreciate my loved ones and those I interact with for who they are without wanting anything or looking to them to fill some needy void in me — to just be able to love them with no strings attached. What joy! What freedom!

Reflecting upon this experience, I realized that experiencing myself as light and sound in the beam at the temple was truly wonderful, but it was not that alone which brought about the feeling of completeness. It was being inside of Prophet's inner form as the Light and Sound of God that made it so;

with him and in him I lack nothing. Here I found I had everything I could ever need: peace, rest and relief, comfort, joy, love, safety and security, clarity, wisdom, and more. These gifts have added so much abundance, fulfillment, and sweetness to my life! Living life in Prophet's inner presence is very much like living inside the beam of light and sound in God's Temple. My relationship with Prophet is the key that unlocks the secrets to all goodness in life. It is what brings the glories of Heaven into one's everyday reality while still living on this Earth.

# 23

# Heart of God

I sat in the great room of Prophet's house singing HU one winter day with him and a small group of students. He brought us to the beach of a vast inner-world Ocean — the Abode of God. It is not a typical ocean as seen in the physical world. The sand and water are alive with God's Love. The sacredness and reverence I experienced brought me to my knees. I was in the presence of God! Love was flowing sweetly and gently back and forth between me and His Divine Presence. Inside I burned with a desire to serve God and give Him everything. As I breathed the next breath I was caught up inside a great vortex that brought me out into the water. I began to swim and relax in this ocean of love. I felt God's Essence infused in the ocean water — it too was an Aspect of God I was allowed to experience. I felt the gentle rise and fall of the swells, my breaths now in sync with Its rhythm. The swells became like breaths taken by enormous lungs within the Ocean. I was aware of being inside what seemed like a huge rib cage, feeling its diaphragm rising and falling in rhythmic unison with the Ocean's swells.

A large hand came up out of the water and Prophet carefully placed me into it. In it I felt comfort and love. Nothing would ever harm me here. I was safe and secure with Prophet in God's Hand, and exhaled a deep relaxing sigh of relief. God brought us up into His Heart where showers of Light and Sound poured down upon me. It was intense enough it physically pinned me back to the sofa on which my body sat. Suddenly, I felt like I was on a rocket that had blasted off and rose up high, coming to rest in a place of great love. I viewed various outer world scenes from within this beautiful place. Everything I saw had a whitish-blue hue to it. I was shown lands in turmoil with violence and battles, but I was not endangered or impacted by it. I was at peace, safe in the tranquility of the Heart of God. What I experienced were but aspects of God's infinite reality, and it was magnificent! I did not want to leave, but I knew a part of me would always be there.

Since this experience there is greater peace with things as they are in my life and in the world around me. If I gently shift my focus and attention I can connect with that part of me that remained in God's Heart — my true home. Whenever I do this it is like taking a deep breath of Divine Spirit. It relaxes me and puts me in a different frame of mind. I have a broader, higher view of the situation and my surroundings. I also view world circumstances from a different perspective when not entangled in them, coming from a more detached place; not detached in a cold and uncaring way but from a core peace within that is not subject to the surface waves of life. Being at peace myself allows me to stay open to God's Love and inner guidance from Prophet. In doing so I can be used to bless others, perhaps by bringing solace and comfort when violence, threat of war, and chaos make things appear hopeless, frightening, or out of control. And though I may not understand why things happen and even grieve and be saddened when I see tragic loss or destruction, I know it will all be okay because God loves us more than we know, and we are not alone. There is a Divine plan and things will work out; ultimately this will be for the highest good of mankind. I trust this because I know no matter what man thinks or does, God is in charge. I remember the feeling of safety and security being in God's Hand and the immense love I felt being taken into His Heart. This changed me and how I view life because now I know my true home, from where I was first loved into existence, and where I can find ultimate rest in the Divine.

# 24

# Joy of Service

The inner spiritual experiences I have shared in telling my story are truly off-the-charts incredible, and yet they are only a sampling of the blessings and magnificence I have witnessed and testify to herein. There were times I was filled with so much Light and Love I surely would have popped if I did not have a way to say "Thank you" to God and His Prophet for allowing it to be so. Singing HU and being able to send gratitude and thanks as well as love to God for all His blessings gave me this outlet. Since Del first shared HU with me I continued to learn more of the facets and wonders of this beautiful prayer and developed greater appreciation for it each year. Another way I keep from bursting is to allow the precious Divine love that fills me to flow through me to others: family, friends, workmates, people I might happen to meet, and even strangers I never even talk to, just am simply near. I shared earlier how living life in Prophet's inner presence is essentially living within the beam of God's Light and Sound. This is the same beam I saw in the inner heavenly temples I was taken to that originates at the source from within God Himself. I know from my own experience that within this beam is everything one could ever want; within it I am complete. I have no unmet needs or desires; I lack nothing. All the treasures of Heaven are available to me: peace, love, joy, clarity, wisdom, inspiration, laughter and lightness, comfort, security, good judgment and discernment, patience and more. When one is so full of love and has continuous access to so much abundance, Soul's natural instinct is to want to pass some of this on to others. By living life in Prophet's presence I am never separated from this source of all, this fountain of life.

*Agape* is the Greek word for love of the highest order. It is found in the Bible in reference to the kind of love God has for His children — unconditional love. His Love is a selfless kind of love. This is the kind of love I aspire to give to other Souls, other children of God. Selflessness is not martyrdom or not loving yourself in a balanced way, it simply means thinking of one's self a little less and of others more often. This godlike quality allows the desire to do things for others to flow out of one's heart in a natural and spontaneous way; being actively open to opportunities to pass on God's Love.

Occasionally I still have to travel to Washington D.C. for work, about a three-hour drive from my home. Even though it makes for a long day, I don't mind the trip at all as I get to stay involved in interesting projects and see old friends and former coworkers. A few weeks ago I was up there for a late afternoon meeting at the Pentagon. It had been a long day, but I was in my usual good-natured mood. I find life to be an adventure when lived in the presence of the Lord, because with eyes to see, the Hand of God is always at work, and it is nothing short of amazing! There is never just a humdrum, ordinary day. By being consciously aware of

Prophet and staying in his presence, even after a long day of work, I am not depleted but still full. I have a love for life and inner peace, happiness, and joy, and these easily find their way to the surface. On this particular day I was walking through the Pentagon's E-Ring after the meeting as I made my way out of the building. The E-Ring is the outermost of the five rings of the building. It is also where the senior military and civilian leaders of the Defense Department work. One can feel a difference in the air as you walk through these stately wood-paneled corridors dedicated with historical renderings of our nation's history and those who served. The responsibility and weight of the offices these Souls carry is unimaginable for most, especially in these chaotic and uncertain times. I passed by a man as I walked. I looked at him and smiled. "Hello," I said. He politely returned my greeting as he walked passed, but a moment later I heard him say something so I turned around. He said, "That's a really nice smile for so late in the day." I smiled and laughed and said, "Thank you," and walked on. It was a brief and simple exchange, yet as I reflected on it I saw such a beauty in how God's Love through my smile was able to provide some upliftment and who knows what else to this Soul. The fact he commented on my "late in the day smile" touched me. I guess it was not something he normally saw, but I think it was more than the physical smile he was seeing. I believe he was recognizing Prophet's presence and the Love of God that flows through him, through me. I doubt he was conscious of this, but for him to stop and turn around and take a moment from the thoughts he was previously immersed in told me he recognized something out of the ordinary. Soul, the eternal part of him, may have been recognizing the Divine, and he was receptive to the gift from God especially meant for him. He thanked me, but really thanks be to God.

In consciously asking to be a vehicle or instrument for God and then surrendering this request, I allow Prophet to use me as a distributor of God's Love. In doing this I can be used to be a blessing to others in whatever way he guides me to share, maybe through a kind word, giving comfort or solace to someone who is hurting, holding the door for someone, giving a hug, listening to someone who needs to talk something out, or a smile. There are infinite ways God's Love can bless others. Everywhere I go I have the opportunity to carry the Light of the World with me in the form of the inner Prophet. This is both a privilege and a joy. I have been blessed with so much, there is no way I could contain it or keep it all to myself. It just overflows and ripples forward in my thoughts, words, and actions, and it is the most natural and satisfying thing in the world.

I used to spend a lot of time walking around in a daze of thoughts, woes, hurts, anxieties of the day, regrets from the past, and worries of the future. Being out of the moment like this was really being self-absorbed because I was focused almost always on me. Many experiences in life are greatly diminished by making them about oneself. When truly present, not merely physically there, I can listen better and be more sensitive to the needs of others. I have found the splendor of living is best experienced being present in the moment and in being more selfless. By God's Grace through His Prophet my heart and my life have been transformed. I have grown from a heart soured on selfish love to one that delights in service. A desire to be used to be a blessing to others burns inside, and I aspire to embody the selflessness of God whose seed has germinated in the rich, tilled soil of my heart today. I find joy in service and I am happiest giving of myself motivated by the pure love of it, not out of neediness looking for something in return. I get it now. I understand why Lynne served Del's coffee with such joy. Service is the reward. A life of loving service is simply sweeter.

# 25

# Hunger Fulfilled

God's Love for Soul infuses our very nature and is part of who we are as His beloved children — to love and be loved. Loving God back with all my heart and all I am brings fulfillment to what I only knew earlier in my life as a longing deep within; the root or reason for I did not know. I think back to that gnawing desire I did not think had anything to do with God or spiritual matters. It was a longing for "something more" I could only chase after in vain through outer means. I thought I was just a restless type with a wild hair, never happy with things as they were. But I know differently now. When I met Del all those years ago he began to teach me about the nature of God and of my true nature as Soul. Over time I learned this longing was for something the outer material world could never satisfy. Everything in the physical is temporary, and though I was not aware of it at the time, what I longed for was something more lasting that would always be. I began to value and be nourished by eternal truth and the inner spiritual world he helped me experience. I came to recognize a loving personal relationship with God and His Prophet was the "more" I sought.

After twenty-two beautiful, life-enriching years as Prophet Del Hall's student, I was given an experience that revealed still more about this longing within. I was seated in class with other spiritual students as we sang HU. My single-minded focus was to send love and give thanks to God through singing this love song. I thought of my Heavenly Father and how I love His Ways. His Word is music to my ears. I thought of how much I love His Son, and how grateful I am that He continues to send us His Prophets throughout eternity to teach us in the physical. I know from experience I am spiritually lost without Prophet showing me the way home to God. Even with the best of intentions there are just too many pitfalls and traps along the way, and I would be blind without a guide who is wise to them. Simply being in Prophet's presence on the inner, or like this day physically being with him, is a privilege and a blessing I have come to appreciate and cherish. As my personal testimony shows, a genuine relationship with Prophet does not happen overnight. It develops naturally through the years and, if nurtured and respected, gradually a very sacred loving relationship emerges. It is because of our priceless relationship my dearest dream as Soul became possible.

I sang HUUUUUU. My eyes closed, I journeyed inward with Prophet through the Heavens and the many spiritual planes to a place where God Himself resided. Too infinite to experience the Allness of the Divine, I was shown one aspect of this Great Being seated in a chair — I was drawn to Him. On my knees before God I swam in indescribable bliss. I was so happy being at the feet of the Almighty singing love and praise to Him. Doing so satisfied an innate desire so core to my being, as if programmed into my DNA. The world would have you think being humble before God and giving praise and glory to Him is a lowly act, but I found it brought rest, satisfied my deepest hunger, and was a cause for rejoicing. I felt more alive and more me than ever!

I turned and looked behind me over my left shoulder and saw my lower self's earthly desire that used to negatively influence and control my life; then I turned back to the Lord God saying, "I want this more." My vision was filled with an all-encompassing brilliant white light. I saw Prophet's strong arm reach out to me — he had been there the whole time. He gently took my hand and walked me into the welcoming Light of God. It felt like I was coming home to where I was first created, from the source of love itself — God's Heart. In this homecoming I had the sense a new chapter in my journey had begun. A quiet solidness filled me, one that comes from knowing who you really are and being confident in what is most important to you. As I came back into my physical body following this experience, I had a stronger love and commitment to God than before and a deeper desire than ever to serve Him. There are two great commandments given in the Bible, "Thou shalt love the Lord thy God with all thy heart, and with all thy soul, and with all thy mind." and, "Thou shalt love thy neighbor as thyself." (Matthew 22:37, 39 KJV). My spiritual journey with Prophet continues to be the grandest adventure of lifetimes for now I know true love, and I know my heart's true desire; it is to make these two great commandments a reality. Glory be to God!

# Post Script

The dictionary defines the word "ideal" as something existing only in one's imagination; desirable or perfect but not likely to become a reality. On one hand I agree with this definition, but from another perspective I do not. I believe there is a certain form of ideal we can make a reality, with help. For many years I carried a shadowy concept of what was ideal in my mind. My life was less about living and truly loving and more of an exhaustive search for this perceived perfection. I force-fit situations and relationships to conform to the rigidity of this unyielding mental mold. This led my life into disarray and brought nothing more than unhappiness, lack of peace, and endless want. But there was more going on. While my mind held this illusory form of an ideal, for which I searched the outer world in vain only to find dead ends, my heart held a promise which led me to freedom. In God I found the True Ideal… perfection!

My story is about how I was taught to make God a reality in my life by drawing nigh and developing a close, personal relationship with Him, living every day in the Light and Sound of God. This makes the true ideal He is a reality. And to His children He endowed a great inheritance, His Divine Essence. This is our personal form of "ideal" to which we can aspire, but it is not embodied in the circumstances or conditions of life, it is within. Our true ideal, not the lower mental facsimile I mistakenly held, is a state of being when we live as Soul, the real us. One of my favorite passages in scripture tells us that if we want to be sure of something and know truth we must look inside our hearts; for if we look outside of ourselves to the outer world, it will only lead to confusion. If we wish to know what direction our life should take, find happiness and love, or have abundance in life, then we must seek the Divine within. This journey within can be tricky though, rather impossible, if on our own. Knowing what I know now, having travelled this road a ways, I would no more recommend going it alone than I would climb Mt. Everest without an experienced and qualified guide; an expert who knows the best route to the summit on that exact day, under those circumstances, for that specific individual, because every situation is different. There is no one-size-fits-all when it comes to one's spiritual wellbeing and journey through life.

By far, the greatest blessing bestowed upon me has been the Grace of God that led me to Del Hall and our sacred relationship that has come to be. In finding him I found an expert, a true Prophet of God. He helped me recognize myself as Soul and manifest the amazing and beautiful God-given qualities I am made of — and you are made of too! I not only discovered the real me but also came to love and respect myself. I stopped wishing I was like someone else and came to appreciate my own individuality, a unique and special blend of "spices" God intentionally created when He made me. Del taught me the ways of God, and I came to see how living in accordance with these

Divine ways was really living in accordance with my own Divine nature, because after all I am created in God's image. I found following God's ways to be a simple recipe for true happiness, peace, and contentment. These include: following fundamental spiritual guidelines and principles, getting daily spiritual nourishment through spiritual exercises, contemplation, reading scripture, nurturing my relationship with Prophet, and living in his inner presence, having a grateful heart, singing HU — a song of love, thanks and praise to God, recognizing and giving thanks for the many gifts of love each day, and joyfully giving of myself in service.

In my heart there has always been a kind of knowing, a seed of wisdom that said *there is more*. It continues to call me forward, chapter by chapter through my still unfolding story. I believe a seed like this was placed in each and every Soul by God when He first created us so that one day, when it is time the ancient wisdom contained in the seed will be stirred awake as it was in me. And like a salmon programmed to go back to the waters of its birth, another cherished Soul will discover in its heart a desire for God and turn towards Home. While the road I travelled may appear to have been broken and winding, it was only that way on the surface. Look deeper still, and see it was a purposeful and sacred path that led me to God. Look deeper still and you may see the sacredness of your own path, and that you too, dear Soul, are a beloved child of God destined someday for your Heavenly Home.

# Guidance for a Better Life
## Our Story

✑✐

## My Father's Journey

God always has a living Prophet on Earth to teach His Ways and accomplish His will. My father, Del Hall III, is currently God's true Prophet fully raised up and ordained by God Himself. He was not always a Prophet, nor did he even know

Prophet Del Hall III

what a Prophet was, but God had a plan for him like He has for all of His children. Over many years through many life experiences, God had begun to prepare my father for his future assignment, mostly unbeknownst to him. Everything he experienced in his life from the joys to the sadness helped prepare him for his future role as Prophet.

My dad grew up in California and was a decent student but a better athlete. He received an appointment to the United States Naval Academy in Annapolis, Maryland where he later met my mother. They were married two days after he graduated and received his commission as an officer. After a short tour on a Navy ship deployed to Vietnam, he went to flight training school and became a Navy fighter pilot. While attending flight school in Pensacola, Florida he also earned a Master of Science Degree and had the first of his three children, a son. After flight school he was stationed in a fighter squadron on the East Coast, where he and my mom began investing in real estate, adding to their family with the birth of two daughters. Following this tour of duty he was assigned as a jet flight instructor in Texas, after which, his time in the Navy was finished. He was a natural pilot and loved his time in the sky, but it was time to move on.

So far in life he had no real concern for, or even thought much about God, religion, or spiritual matters in general. He lived life fully. He raised his family. He traveled. He invested and became an entrepreneur starting and growing highly successful businesses in diverse fields ranging from real estate to aerospace consulting. Years before however, a seed had been planted when God's eternal teachings were introduced to him in his late teens, and while it did not show outwardly, the truth in these teachings spoke to his heart. My dad might not have been giving much thought about God up to this point in his life, but God was definitely thinking about him and the future He had planned for him. Like an acorn destined to become a mighty oak, the seed that lay dormant in his heart would someday be stirred to life. Through all his life experiences, both "good" and "bad," God would be preparing him for his future role as His Prophet.

When God decided it was time, He called my dad to Him. He did this by shutting down the world of financial security my dad had built. Over a period of two years all of his businesses were wound down and dissolved. What seemed like security turned out to be an illusion. Financial success had not provided true security. He now had failed businesses and a failing marriage and was trying to fix things without God's help, principles, or guidance. As painful as this time in his life was, it was yet another step towards the glorious life of service awaiting my father. God was removing him from the world my dad had created and furthering him along his path to his future role as Prophet.

After his marriage ended and his businesses wound down, he started fresh by going out west to give flying lessons near Lake Mead, Nevada. While living in Nevada my dad was reintroduced to the eternal teachings of God he first learned of as a teenager twenty-three years earlier, and though they resonated with him at the time, his priorities were different back then. Now, his serious training could begin. He started having very clear experiences with the Holy

Spirit and noticed there was a familiarity with these teachings and experiences. He embraced the long hours of instruction, which often lasted until sunrise, and was receptive to the personal spiritual experiences he was given. This began an intense period of study and desire for spiritual truth that continues to this day. Some of his most profound and meaningful experiences during this time were with past Prophets of old. They came to him spiritually in contemplations and dreams. He learned of their roles in history and how they were raised up and ordained by God directly. He began to realize they were training him but was not clear why. A few times his experiences led him to believe he was in training to be a future Prophet. However, that revelation made no sense to him because he felt he was an imperfect person who made mistakes and had failures. He thought of the past and current Prophets of God as perfected Souls, not imperfect like he felt he was. Why would God choose him for such a role? He did not feel qualified.

Besides being introduced to God's teachings while he was out west, my father was blessed to meet his current wife Lynne. Returning to the East Coast, my father and Lynne moved into a small cabin on land he had acquired before his businesses shut down. This was a major change in his life, but it felt deeply right within him. He began to remember a desire to live like this as a child; from early childhood my dad found clarity and peace in nature. He had forgotten about this until now, but God had not and made this dream a reality. In addition to being their home, these beautiful, three-hundred-plus acres of land in the Blue Ridge Mountains would eventually become the location for the Guidance for a Better Life retreat center. The perfection of my father's experiences from earlier in his life in real estate, providing the land for his next step in life, speaks to the perfection of God's plan. One of many many examples I could list.

For many years my dad took wilderness skills courses around the country. He specialized in the study of wild edible and medicinal plants, tracking, and awareness skills, and authored articles for publication. Inspired to help folks feel more comfortable in the outdoors, my dad and Lynne began the Nature Awareness School in 1990. Classes were focused on teaching awareness and the primitive living skills needed to enjoy the woods and survive in them if necessary. An amazing thing happened within those first few years though; students began to experience aspects of God in very personal and dramatic ways. Somewhat like my dad's experience out west, they found that stepping away from their daily routine and the hustle of life, if even for a few days, created space for Spirit to do Its work. Whether they were enjoying the beauty of the Virginia wilderness and tranquility of the school grounds or relaxing by the pond, he found students' hearts opened, and they became more receptive to the Divine Hand that is always reaching out to Its children. More and more the discourse during wilderness classes shifted to the meanings of dreams, personal growth, finding balance in life, and experiences the students were having with the Voice of God in Its many forms. An increase of spiritual retreats was offered to fulfill the demand and over time became the predominant class offerings; the wilderness survival skills classes eventually fading away completely. The name "Nature Awareness School" seemed to be less fitting for what was actually being taught now and in February 2019 my father changed the name of the retreat center to Guidance for a Better Life.

Throughout this time my father's training and spiritual study continued. My father reached mastership and was ordained by God on July 7, 1999 but he was still not yet Prophet, more was required. On October 22, 2012, twenty-five years since his full-time intensive training had begun, God ordained him as His chosen Prophet, and He has continued to raise him up further since. God works through my father in very direct and beneficial ways for his students. Hundreds and hundreds of students for more than thirty years have received God's eternal teachings through my father's instruction and mentoring. They have had personal experiences with the Divine which have transformed and greatly blessed their lives. My father's greatest joy is being used by God as a servant to share God's ways and truths with thirsty Souls and hungry seekers. In addition to mountaintop retreats, my father continues to spread God's ways and teachings that so greatly blessed his life and the lives of his loved ones in many ways, including his books and videos.

Maybe you are at a turning point in your life and looking for direction. Maybe you have a knowing there is more to life but not sure what that might be or how to find it. Or, maybe you are simply drawn to what you read and hear in our stories. God speaks to our hearts and calls each of us in many different ways. Like my father's journey demonstrates, it doesn't matter where you started or the twists, turns, or seeming dead-ends your life has taken; God wants us to know Him more fully, and for us to know our purpose within His creation. He wants us to experience His Love regardless of our religious path or lack thereof. He always has a living Prophet here on Earth to help us accomplish His desire for us — to show us the way home to Him and to experience more abundance in our lives while we are still living here on Earth. God's Prophet today is my father, Del Hall III. You have the opportunity to grow spiritually through God's teachings which Prophet shares. His guidance for a better life is available for you — please accept it.

Written by Del Hall IV

# My Son, Del Hall IV

My son, Del Hall IV, joined Guidance for a Better Life as an instructor after fifteen years of in-class training with me, his father. He helped develop the five-step Keys to Spiritual Freedom Study Program and facilitates the first two courses in the

Del Hall IV

program: Step One "Tools to Recognize Divine Guidance" and Step Two "Understanding Divine Guidance." Del also teaches people about the rich history of dream study and how to better recall their own dreams during the Dream Study Workshops, which he hosts around the country. He is qualified to step in and

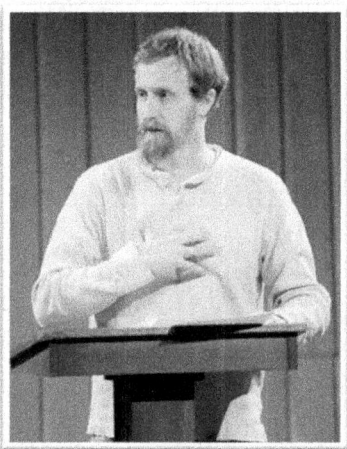

facilitate any of my retreats should the need arise.

Del authored the book *God is in the Garden*, a priceless book of wisdom in the form of parables. Through stories of everyday events of life on the mountain Del shares profound insights into the nature of God and life that are infused with his natural humor and unique perspective.

Del is also Vice President of Marketing and helps with everything required to get the "good news" from Guidance for a Better Life out to hungry seekers: everything from book publishing, blogging, and posting on social media outlets. He is co-author and book cover designer for many of our, thus far, twenty published books.

My son loves the opportunity to work on creative projects for Guidance for a Better Life. From a very early age he has been an artist and loved creating artwork in multiple mediums. He was accepted into gifted art programs in Virginia Beach, Virginia and then after high school graduation he attended the School of the Museum of Fine Arts in Boston.

He is now a nationally exhibited artist and his *Paintings of the Light and Sound of God* are in over two hundred public and private collections. One of the greatest joys of the painting process for Del is using his paintings as an opportunity to share with others the inspiration behind them, God's Love and his experiences with the Light and Sound of God, the Holy Spirit, in contemplation and in waking life.

Del lives on the retreat center property in the Blue Ridge Mountains of Virginia with his wife where they raised and homeschooled my three grandchildren. Recently he helped me with an extensive renovation and update for the three hand-built log cabins on retreat center property originally used for advanced spiritual retreats. He loves woodworking, tending to his vegetable garden, pruning his fruit trees, and helping maintain the beautiful three-hundred acres of retreat center property for students to enjoy. There is always something that needs attention on the land and Del is always up to the challenge. He loves to travel and spends his free time enjoying this beautiful country with his family in their RV.

My son has had multiple brain surgeries starting when he was seventeen years old for a recurring brain tumor. He credits God for surviving and thriving all this time when most with his condition do not. He looks to the sunrise every day with gratitude for yet another chance at life. With that chance he desires to help me share the love and teachings of God that have so blessed our lives. I pray to God daily thanking Him for my son's good health.

Written by Prophet Del Hall

# What is the Role of God's Prophet?

An introductory understanding of God's handpicked and Divinely trained Prophet is necessary to fully benefit from reading this book. God ALWAYS has a living Prophet of His choice on Earth. He has a physical body with a limited number of students, but the inner spiritual side of Prophet is limitless. Spiritually he can help countless numbers of Souls all over the world, no matter what religion or path they are on — even if that is no path at all. He teaches the ways of God and shares the Light and Sound of God. He delivers the living Word of God. Prophet can teach you physically as well as through dreams, and he can lift you into the Heavens of God. He offers protection, peace, teachings, guidance, healing, and love.

Each of God's Prophets throughout history has a unique mission. One may only have a few students with the sole intent to keep

God's teachings and truth alive. God may use another to change the course of history. God's Prophets are usually trained by both the current and former Prophets. The Prophet is tested and trained over a very long period of time. The earlier Prophets are physically gone but teach the new Prophet in the inner spiritual worlds. This serves two main purposes: the trainee becomes very adept at spiritual travel and gains wisdom from those in whose shoes he will someday walk. This is vital training because the Prophet is the one who must safely prepare and then take his students into the Heavens and back.

There are many levels of Heaven, also called planes or mansions. Saint Paul once claimed to know a man who went to the third Heaven. Actually it was Paul himself that went, but the pearl is, if there is a third Heaven, it presumes a first and second Heaven also exist. The first Heaven is often referred to as the Astral plane. Even on just that one plane of existence there are over one hundred sub-planes. This Heaven is where most people go after passing, unless they receive training while still here in their physical body. Without a guide who is trained properly in the ways of God a student could misunderstand the intended lesson and become confused as to what is truth. The inner worlds are enormous compared to the physical worlds. They are very real and can be explored safely when guided by God's Prophet.

Part of my mission is to share more of what is spiritually possible for you as a child of God. Few Souls know or understand that God's Prophet can safely guide God's children, while still alive physically, to their Heavenly Home. Taking a child of God into the Heavens is not the job of clergy. Clergy have a responsibility to pass on the teaching of their religion exactly as they were taught, not to add additional concepts or possibilities. If every clergy member taught their own personal belief system no religion could survive for long. Then the beautiful teachings of an earlier Prophet of God would be lost. Clergy can be creative in finding interesting and uplifting ways to share their teachings, but their job is to keep their religion intact. However, God sends His Prophets to build on the teachings of His past Prophets, to share God's Light and Love, to teach His language, and to guide Souls to their Heavenly Home.

There is ALWAYS MORE when it comes to God's teachings and truth. No one Prophet can teach ALL of God's ways. It may be that the audience of a particular time in history cannot absorb more wisdom. It could be due to a Prophet's limited time to teach and limited time in a physical body on Earth. Ultimately, it is that there is ALWAYS MORE! Each of God's Prophets brings additional teachings and opportunities for ways to draw closer to God, building on the work and teachings of former Prophets. That is one reason why Prophets of the past ask God to send another; to comfort, teach, and continue to help God's children grow into greater abundance. Former Prophets continue to have great love for God's children and want to see them continue to grow in accepting more of God's Love. One never needs to stop loving or accepting help from a past Prophet in order to grow with the help of the current Prophet. All true Prophets of God work together and help one another to do God's work.

All the testimonies in this book were written by students at the Guidance for a Better Life retreat center. It is here that the nature of God, the Holy Spirit, and the nature of Soul are EXPERIENCED under the guidance of a true living Prophet of God. Guidance for a Better Life is NOT a religion, it is a retreat center. God and His Prophet are NOT disparaging of any religion of love. However, the more a path defines itself with its teachings, dogma, or tenets, the more "walls" it inadvertently creates between the seeker and God. Sometimes it even puts God into a smaller box. God does not fit in any box. Prophet is for all Souls and is purposely not officially aligned with any path, but shows respect to all.

YOU can truly have an ABUNDANT LIFE through a personal and loving relationship with God, the Holy Spirit, and God's ordained Prophet. This is my primary message to you. Having a closer relationship with the Divine requires understanding the "Language of the Divine." God expresses His Love to us, His children, in many different and sometimes very subtle ways. Often His Love goes unrecognized and unaccepted because His language is not well known. The testimonies in this book have shown you some of the ways in which God expresses His Love. It is my hope that in reading this book, you have begun to learn more of the "Language of the Divine." The stories spanned from very subtle Divine guidance to profound examples of experiencing God up close and very personal. After reading this book I hope you now know your relationship with God has the potential to be more profound, more personal, and more loving than any organized religion on Earth currently teaches.

If you wish to develop a relationship with God's Prophet, seek the inner side of Prophet, for he is spiritually already with you.

Few are able to meet the current physical incarnation and most people do not need to meet Prophet physically. Gently sing HU for a few minutes and then sing "Prophet" with love in your heart and he will respond. It may take time to recognize his presence, but it will come. The Light and Love that flows through him is the same that has flowed through all of God's true Prophets.

A more abundant life awaits you,

Prophet Del Hall III

# HU — An Ancient Name For God

HU is an ancient name for God that can be sung quietly or aloud in prayer. HU has existed since the beginning of time in one form or another and is available to all regardless of religion. It is a pure way to express your love to God and give thanks for your blessings.

Singing HU (HUUUUUU pronounced "hue") serves as a tuning fork with Spirit that brings you into greater harmony with the Divine. We recommend singing HU a few minutes each day. This can bring love, joy, peace, and clarity, or help you rise to a higher view of a situation when upset or fearful.

# Articles of Faith

Written by Prophet Del Hall III

1. There is one true God who is still living and active in our lives. He is knowable and wants a relationship with each of His children. He is the same God Jesus called FATHER and is known by many names, including Heavenly Father, and the ancient names for God, HU, and Sugmad (Pronounced SOOG-mahd). God wants a loving, trusting, personal relationship with each of us, NOT one based upon fear or guilt.

2. The Holy Spirit is God's expression in all the worlds. It is in two parts, the Light and the Sound. It is through His Holy Spirit God communicates and delivers all His gifts: peace, clarity, love, joy, healings, correction, guidance, wisdom, comfort, truth, dreams, new revelations, and more.

3. God always has a chosen living Prophet to teach His ways, speak His Living Word, lift up

Souls, and bring us closer to God. God's living Prophet is a concentrated aspect of the Holy Spirit, the Light and Sound, and is raised up and ordained by God directly. His Prophet is empowered and authorized to share God's Light and Sound and to correct misunderstandings of His ways. There are two aspects of God's Prophet, an inner spiritual and outer physical Prophet. The inner Prophet can teach us through dreams, intuition, spiritual travel, inner communication, and his presence. The outer Prophet also teaches through his discourses, written word, and his presence. There is no separation between the inner and outer Prophet. Both inner and outer aspects of Prophet are concentrated aspects of the Holy Spirit. Prophet is always with us spiritually on the inner. Prophet points to and glorifies the Father.

4. God so loves the world and His children He has always had a long unbroken line of His chosen Prophets on Earth. They existed before Jesus and after Jesus. Jesus was God's Prophet and His actual SON. God's

chosen Prophets are considered to be in the "role of God's son," though NOT literally His Son. Only Jesus was literally His Son. Prophets were sometimes called Paraclete. The Bible uses the word Comforter, but the original Greek word was Paraclete, which is more accurate. Paraclete implies an actual physical person who helps, counsels, encourages, advocates, comforts, sets free, and more.

5. Our real and eternal self is called Soul. We are Soul; we do NOT "have" a Soul. As Soul we are literally an individualized piece of God's Holy Spirit, thereby divine in nature. As an individual and uniquely experienced Soul you have free will, intelligence, imagination, opinions, clear and continuous access to Divine guidance, and immortality. As Soul we have an innate and profound spiritual growth potential. Soul has the ability to travel the Heavens spiritually with Prophet to gain truth and wisdom and grow in love. Soul exists because God loves It.

6. We have one eternal life as Soul. However, Soul needs to incarnate many times into a

physical body to learn and grow spiritually mature. Soul's long journey back home to God where It was first created encompasses many lifetimes. A loving God does not expect His children to learn His ways in a single lifetime.

7. Soul equals Soul, in that God loves all Souls equally and each Soul has the same innate qualities and potential. Soul is neither male nor female, any particular race, nationality, or age. When Soul comes into a physical body at birth, the physical body is male or female, a certain race, a nationality, and has an age. All Souls are children of God. We do not have to earn God's Love; He loves us unconditionally.

8. Soul incarnates on Earth to grow in the ability to give and receive love and learn to live the way God wishes us to live. Because God loves us, His ways of living create abundant, happy, fulfilling lives. His beautiful ways of living are mostly HOW to live, and less on what NOT to do.

9. God is more interested in two Souls learning to love one another regardless of their sexual preference. God loves you just the way you are.

10. It is God's will that a negative power exists to help Soul grow spiritually through challenges and hardships, thereby strengthening and maturing Soul. We are never given a challenge greater than our ability to find a solution to or understand the necessary lesson, if we use our God-given creativity, make sufficient personal effort, and ask for and accept the help available from the Divine. Soul has the ability to rise above any obstacles with God's help.

11. We study the Bible as an authentic teaching tool of God's ways, in addition to books and discourses authored by a Prophet chosen by God. We know the original biblical writings are sometimes misunderstood, for example, God loves each of us regardless of our errors and shortcomings. God's eternal abandonment or damnation is not true. He would never turn His back to us for eternity. (Isaiah 54:7-8

and 10, Lamentations 3:31-32, and Hebrews 13:5)

12. Karma is the way in which the Divine accounts for our actions, words, thoughts, and attitudes. One can create positive or negative karma. Karma is a blessing used to teach us responsibility.

13. A child is not born in sin, however, the child does have karma from former lives. Karma, God's accounting system, explains our birth circumstances better than the concept of sin.

14. A living Prophet, including Jesus, can remove karma and sin when necessary to help us get started or to grow on the path home to God. However, it is primarily our responsibility to live and grow in the ways of God, thereby not creating negative karma and sin.

15. There are four commandments of God in which we abide: First — Love God with all your heart, mind, and Soul; Second — Love your neighbor as yourself. The Third is, "Seek ye first the Kingdom of God, and His

righteousness." This means that it is primarily our responsibility to draw close to God, learn His ways, and strive to live the way God would like us to live. God's Prophet is sent to show His ways. Our purpose, the Fourth Commandment, is to become spiritually mature to be used by God to bless His children. Becoming a coworker with God through His Comforter is our primary purpose in life and the most rewarding attainment of Soul.

16. All Souls upon translation, death of the physical body, go to the higher worlds, called Heavens, planes, or mansions, regardless of their beliefs. The way they live life on Earth and the effort made to draw close to God impacts the area of Heaven they are to be sent. Those who purposely harm others (except in defense of self or others), themselves, or live against the ways of God go to unpleasant locations on the first Heaven; to a location where they can learn how to do better, as a gift of love. The first Heaven has a wide range of locations, from very very unpleasant and hellish, to

wonderful and beautiful places to spend time with loved ones while learning and preparing for future incarnations. Those who draw close to a Prophet of God, including Jesus, receive special care. We know of twelve distinct Heavens, not one. The primary Abode of the Heavenly Father is in the twelfth Heaven, known as the Ocean of Love and Mercy. We can visit God while we still live on Earth, if taken by His chosen Prophet and only as Soul, not in a physical body.

17. Prayer is sacred, personal exchange with God and is an extreme privilege. God hears every prayer from the heart whether or not we recognize a response. Singing an ancient name of God, HU, is our foundational prayer. It expresses love and gratitude to God and is unencumbered by words. Singing HU has the potential to raise us up in consciousness making us more receptive to God's Love, Light, and guiding Hand. After praying it is best to spend time listening to God. Prayer should never be rote or routine. We desire to trust God and to know His will for us, and then freely and joyfully surrender to His will

rather than our own will. God's Prophet can teach us the "Language of the Divine" which will help us understand how God communicates with us and help us recognize God's Love in our lives.

18. It is our responsibility to stay spiritually nourished. When Soul is nourished and fortified It becomes activated, and we are more receptive and have clearer communication with the Divine. When Jesus said, "Give us this day our daily bread," he meant daily spiritual nourishment, not physical bread. The Holy Spirit is nourishment for Soul. This can be received by singing HU, studying Scripture, praying, dream study, demonstrating gratitude for our blessings, being in a living Prophet's physical presence or in his inner presence, or listening to his words.

19. TRUTH has the power to improve every area of our lives, but only if understood, accepted, and integrated into our lives.

20. God and His Prophet guide us in our sleeping dreams and awake dreams as a gift

of love. God's Prophet teaches how to understand both types of dreams. All areas of our lives may be blessed by the wisdom God offers each of us directly in dreams.

21. Gratitude is extremely important on the path of love. It is literally the secret of love. Developing an attitude of gratitude is necessary to becoming spiritually mature. Recognizing and being grateful for the blessings of God in our lives is vital to building a loving and trusting relationship with God and His chosen Prophet. A relationship with God's Prophet is THE KEY to everything good. This includes a more abundant life filled with the Treasures of Heaven Jesus taught about in Matthew 6.

22. We are to be good stewards of our blessings. We recognize them as gifts of love from God and make the effort to have remembrance. Remembering our blessings helps to keep our hearts open to God and builds trust in God's Love for us.

23. We give others the respect and freedom to have their own beliefs, make their own

choices, and live their lives as they wish. We expect the same in return.

24. The Love and blessings of God and His Prophet are available to all who are receptive. If one desires guidance and help from Prophet, ask from the heart and sing "Prophet." He will respond. One does not need to meet Prophet physically to receive help because he is a concentrated aspect of God's Holy Spirit, and is always with us. To be taught by Prophet in the physical is a sacred blessing. Much can be gained by reading or listening to the Heavenly Father's teachings being shared by Prophet.

25. We have a responsibility to do our part and let God and His Prophet do their part. This responsibility brings freedom. Our goal is to remain spiritually nourished, live the ways of God, live in balance with a core peace, and serve God as a coworker through His Comforter. We pray to use our God-given free will in a way that our actions, thoughts, words, and attitudes testify and bear witness to the Glory and Love of God.

26. There is always more to learn and grow in God's ways and truth. One cannot remain the same spiritually. One must make the effort to move forward or risk falling backward. To grow in consciousness and love requires change. Spiritual wisdom gained during our earthly incarnations can be taken to the other worlds when we translate, and into future lifetimes, unlike our physical possessions that remain in the physical.

# Contact Information

Guidance for a Better Life is a worldwide mentoring program provided by Prophet Del Hall III and his son Del Hall IV. Personal one-on-one mentoring at our retreat center is our premier offering and the most direct and effective way to grow spiritually. Spiritual tools, guided exercises, and in-depth discourses on the eternal teachings of God are provided to help one become more aware of and receptive to His Holy Spirit and the abundance that awaits. With this personally-tailored guidance one begins to more fully recognize God's Love daily in their lives, both the dramatic and the very subtle. Over time our mentoring reduces fear, worry, anxiety, lack of purpose, feelings of unworthiness, guilt, and confusion; replacing those negative aspects of life with an abundance of peace, clarity, joy, wisdom, love, and self-respect leading to a more personal relationship with God, more than most know is possible. We also offer our videos, and more than twenty inspirational and educational books.

**Guidance for a Better Life**

P.O. Box 219

Lyndhurst, Virginia 22952

(540) 377-6068

contact@guidanceforabetterlife.com

www.guidanceforabetterlife.com

If you could only read one of Prophet Del Hall's books this is the one. It is full of Keys to unlock the treasures of Heaven and bring more of God's Love into your life.

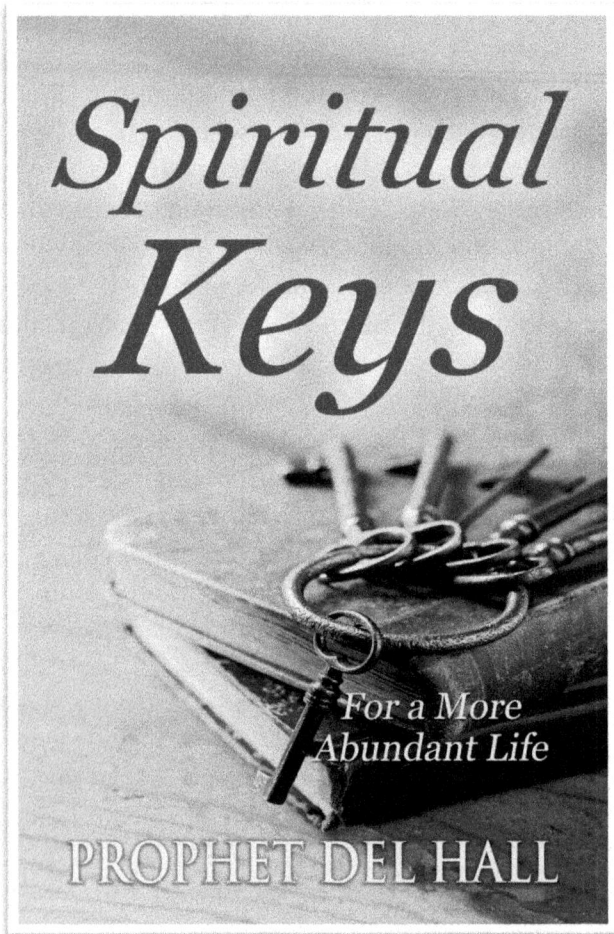

*Spiritual*

*Keys*

For a More
Abundant Life

PROPHET DEL HALL

Wayshowers are God's special emissaries to Earth. Our Heavenly Father loves us so much He has never left us alone without a Wayshower to teach us His true ways. This book explores the amazing history of God's chosen and ordained Wayshowers from thirty-five thousand years ago to today through specific examples of both well-known and little-known Wayshowers.

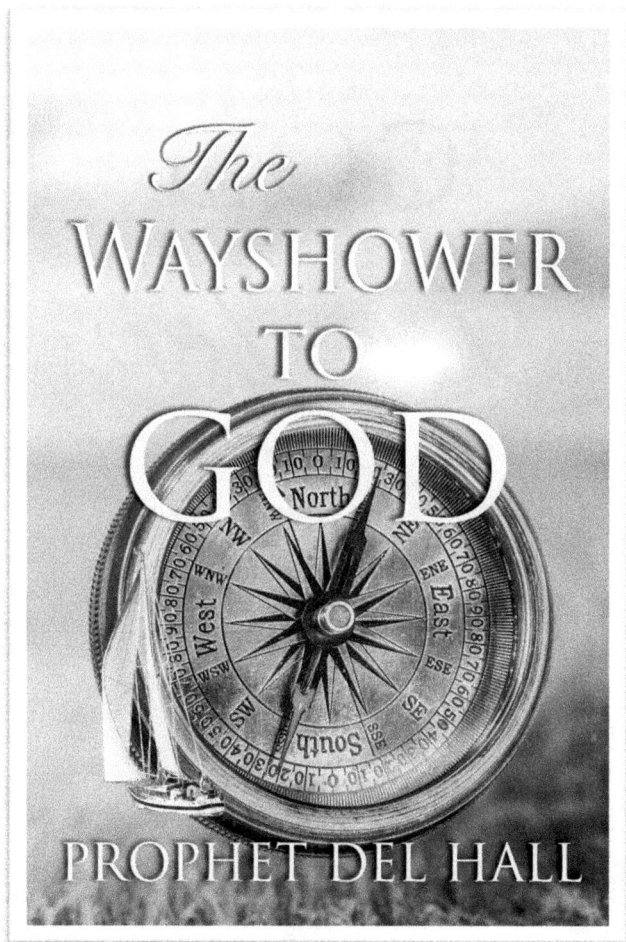

*The* WAYSHOWER TO GOD

PROPHET DEL HALL

## GOD IS IN THE GARDEN
## PARABLES

Regardless of what your venture is in life you can benefit from this unassuming book. It may appear small, but the parables contained within have the power to affect your life in extraordinary ways.

# GOD
IS IN THE
## Garden

## PARABLES
## BY DEL HALL IV

# ZOOM WITH PROPHET

Guidance for a Better Life retreat center has been hosting in-person mountaintop retreats at our beautiful location in the Blue Ridge Mountains of Virginia since 1990. When the pandemic began in 2020, it inspired us to get creative with how to connect with our students and new seekers. It was then our *Zoom With Prophet* meeting series was born. Some of these Zoom meetings are now being put into book form for those who could not attend.

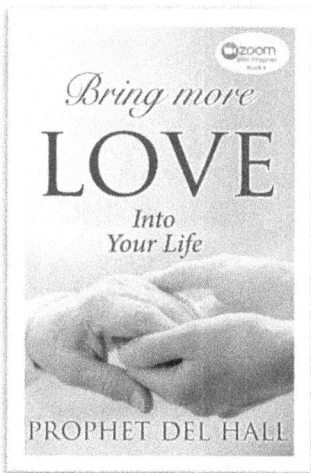

## SPECIALIZED TOPICS

Whether you wish to reconnect with a loved one who has passed, understand how you too can experience God's Light, improve your marriage, or learn how to understand your dreams, these incredible books have you covered.

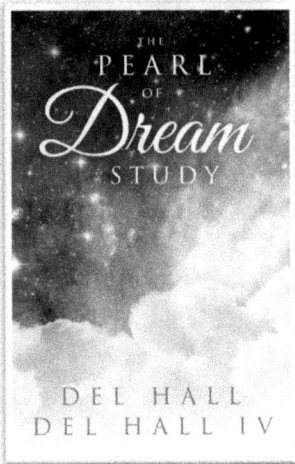

# TESTIMONIES OF GOD'S LOVE SERIES

God expresses His Love every day in many different and sometimes subtle ways. Often this love goes unrecognized because the ways in which God communicates are not well known. Each of the books in this series contains fifty true stories that will help you learn to better recognize the Love of God in your life.

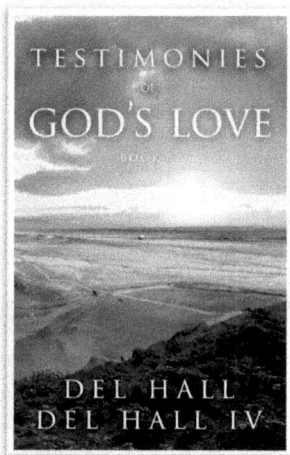

# JOURNEY TO A TRUE SELF-IMAGE SERIES

This series includes intimate and unique stories that many readers will be able to personally identify with, enjoy, and learn from. They will help the reader transcend the false images people often carry about themselves — first and foremost that they are only their physical mind and body. The authors share their journeys of recognizing and coming to more fully accept their true self-image, that of Soul — an eternal child of God.

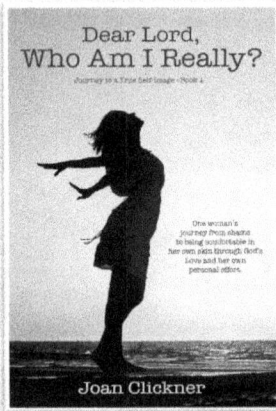

Dear Lord, Who Am I Really?
Joan Clickner

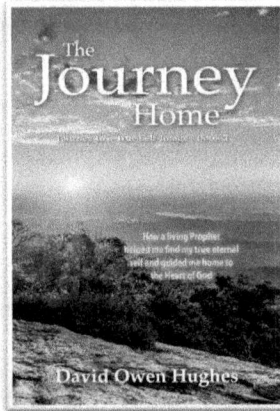

The Journey Home
David Owen Hughes

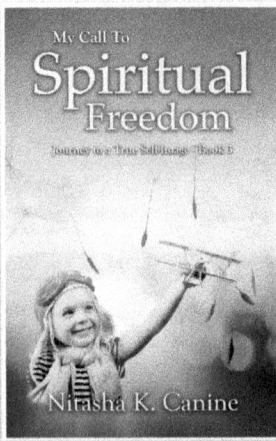

My Call To Spiritual Freedom
Nitasha K. Canine

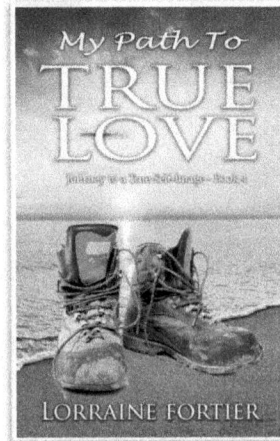

My Path To True Love
Lorraine Fortier